JOE'S VIOLIN

A Survivor Remembers

JOSEPH FEINGOLD

Joseph Feingold
c/o Rachen Press
305 West End Ave., Suite 1207
New York, NY 10023

ISBN: 978-1986172998

Book design by 52 Novels
http://www.52novels.com

DEDICATION

This book is dedicated in loving memory of my wife, Regina Kaufman Feingold; my mother Ruchele and father Aron, and especially, my little brother Henryk, who perished at Treblinka.

This book is in tribute to the courageous members of my family and all those whose lives were cut short by the infamous events of WWII and the Holocaust. May their lives be remembered.

Joe's Violin film poster.

CONTENTS

*Jozef, second from right, his brothers Alex, Henryk,
and parents Rachel and Aaron, Kielce, Poland, 1936.*

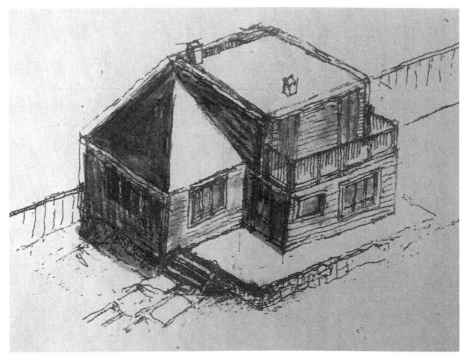

Joe's sketch of his house in Kielce, based on copies of construction plans received from a historian in Warsaw. Joe filled in missing parts based on memory.

Zeilsheim Displaced Persons Camp, Winter, 1946

I never could have imagined that my choice in 1946 to purchase a violin instead of a winter coat, would change my life. But it did. A short film called *Joe's Violin*, made in 2014, told the story of how I bought a violin at a flea market while living in a German Displaced Persons (DP) Camp. Almost 70 years later, I donated that violin through an instrument drive to a public school in the South Bronx.

After World War II, I was living with hundreds of mostly Jewish survivors, including my father and brother Alex, in Zeilsheim, just outside of Frankfurt. The winter days were bitter cold. The logical thing to buy would've been cheap winter clothes. But when I spotted the violin, its dark red wood gleaming in the frozen sunshine, something in me stirred. I had to have it. I paid a German man for the violin in a simple barter, with a carton of American cigarettes. I clutched my new instrument and walked past the stalls stacked with warm coats and fur hats. Holding it, the violin warmed my soul, if not my body, and memories flooded my mind.

There I was in the cozy apartment on Zhelasna Street in Warsaw, always full of music and company. I could hear every note of the songs my mother sang to us. It had been my parents' idea for their children to play an instrument. I was not more than five when I got my first violin. I played it until 1939 when, as Jews, we were forced to flee Warsaw. Seven years later, the flea market violin filled me with longing and sorrow, but also with the joy of those happier memories.

I knew I had made the right purchase, even though the violin's true significance would not become fully apparent for decades, until after the film was made.

I often wonder, *How did this film come to be?* It started by accident after a filmmaker heard on the radio how I got my violin in Germany so long ago. She wanted to meet me and she did. After a time, she made the film, *Joe's Violin,* which brings together so many melodies of my life, from melancholy to joyful.

The filmmaker, Kahane Cooperman, would not have heard my story if I hadn't heard of an instrument drive while listening to WQXR, the classical music radio station. The radio announcer was asking people to donate musical instruments they no longer played to New York City schoolchildren. *I can do that!* I thought. It seemed like the perfect solution. I lifted the dusty case in the corner, and took a bus with the violin to the collection point for the instruments at Lincoln Center.

The person at WQXR who received my instrument was fascinated by its story: "I paid for the violin with a carton of cigarettes. I think I did pretty well," I said, describing the transaction at the flea market. The drive was so successful, that over 2,000 instruments jammed every corner of that storage room. I was surprised to find out my remarks were aired on the radio, and that's why I received a call from Kahane soon after she heard the story over her car radio.

Wondering what kind of man gets a fiddle from a German guy in a flea market and donates it to a school, she tracked me down and soon she began filming me. My wife was very ill at the time, but she filmed her too. Unfortunately, Regina died in October, 2015. She didn't get to see the complete film, but she is in a scene.

Meanwhile, the violin had made its way to the Bronx Global Learning Institute for Girls in the South Bronx. At this amazing school, each student is given a violin to play starting in kindergarten and through to eighth grade graduation. One of the school's music teachers, Kokoe Tanaka-Suwan, had selected Brianna Perez, then 12, to receive the violin. She wrote me a beautiful letter of thanks, inviting me to visit the school. So I went from my apartment, with Kahane and Ame, to the South Bronx.

When I met Brianna, it was so special. A chord was struck. We shared a common bond, a love for music and this violin. She understood its history, the legacy she held in her hands. I felt fortunate that my violin had found her. I don't want to give away too much from the film, but in it Brianna says, "My life is playing the violin."

Brianna graduated Bronx Global (BGLIG) and began music studies at a prestigious high school. The violin was passed down to a younger student, Nya, and then to Sasha. When one student graduates, it goes to the next one.

Joe's Violin was first shown on April 3, 2016, at my residence on West End Avenue. Some 80 friends, neighbors, and family came. After the screening, Brianna played the violin and some students, Kokoe and another music teacher, Hannah van der Swaagh, played other instruments.

The next week, the film was released and shown at the Tribeca Film Festival and several other festivals. It got a lot of media attention, including on TV, WQXR, in American and Israeli newspapers, and in The New Yorker and other magazines. You will read more about this later.

But the biggest surprise was yet to come.

In November, 2016, I received a call that *Joe's Violin* had been nominated for an Academy Award in the best short documentary film category. It had made it to the final round of five nominated films. I couldn't believe it.

Brianna, her mother, Mercedes, Kahane, Raphaela Neihausen, the producer, and Kokoe, went to the Oscars in Hollywood in February, 2017.

I stayed home. The scene would've been a bit too much for a man of my age. I would've had to buy new clothes and get all dressed up. They all had a blast even though we didn't win. Brianna brought me back photos, memorabilia, and an authentic program book from the Oscars.

I often think about the choice I made at the flea market. I didn't give away the violin because it didn't mean anything. I gave it away because it meant so much.

The radio announcement in 2014 and events that followed continue to have an astonishing effect on my life in ways I could never have predicted. The violin I've loved for over 70 years still touches hearts as people watch the film around the country and abroad.

None of this would have happened had my mother not given me my first violin when I was a carefree child, instilling her love of music in me for the rest of my life.

A MUSICAL PRELUDE

My mother ignited in me a love for all music. I enjoyed classical music, or as I knew it in Poland, serious music. I also loved Jewish songs, especially as sung by my mother. Another great interest was films, particularly French films—not permitted to be viewed by youngsters like me. My parents, with limited funds, bought me a violin, and later, one for my brother, a small violin which I played constantly from the age of five. Although I derived a lot of pleasure from it, more so when accompanied by my mother's singing, I don't think I got much better in playing this beautiful instrument. I always managed to have my violin with me, except for the six years I spent in Siberia.

I recall the violin of my youth as a rather intimate extension of my body. Each string has a special personality. G was stern like a grandfather. D was tolerant like my father and supportive of my mother, the A string—a favorite tone I relied on, well, as did my mother. The E string was difficult, like a very young daughter, sometimes serious and so demanding, with flights up and up and then slightly down. I didn't manage that one too well. I wasn't very successful with girls.

Life evolved for me from happy childhood to trying times, war, Siberia, being nearly killed, and finally achieving full freedom and happiness. I was fighting for survival and persistently running and reappearing from 1939 to 1946 and the years beyond. In writing this memoir, I am hoping to share my lost and regained memories with you and impart in some measure the elements that have sustained me all these years.

Rachel (Ruchele) and Aaron (Aron) Fajngold.

Rachel and Aaron.

New Beginnings

Monday, February 18, 1985.

Sitting in my office, I start to record my memoir for the first time. I am 61 years old, a proud American, married (finally!), surrounded by many people whom I care for deeply, and who care for me. I'm a happy man who "made it." And yet… my memory carries a burden more than half a century old: it has ugly scar tissue or, rather, deep raw wounds which will never heal.

I must say that my family, with my wife Regina, and her children Ame and Karen, and later my grandchildren, added a dimension to my life which I had never experienced before, although I knew intellectually that it existed. They also opened up a new meaning to my life which inspired me to record my memoirs. They loved me and I loved them. They wanted to know more about me. They asked me questions about my past. I delighted in telling them bits and pieces from my life. To them it was fascinating, and also very foreign.

I cannot help but think about my brother Alex's three kids. I don't know how much they know about their father's life. What I do know is that it would be a great deprivation for them not to know about it. I can see how one could shield someone from sad or cruel experiences up to a point, though beyond that it works to the detriment of a person's own emotional growth. So this too may be one of the reasons why I wanted my life to be recorded.

I started to write my memoir in 1985. The impetus was Ame, my younger daughter by marriage. When she was a student at Elizabeth Irwin High School (in the 1970s), she invited me to tell her classmates about my life. I was thrilled by the idea that there were people interested in my story, and I was moved by their response. I discovered that everyone in the class was also moved, for their own personal reasons. To them it was a revelation; though it depicted a life so foreign to their experience, it gave meaning to material that they discussed in school about the Second World War, extermination of a people, separation of families, the concept of anti-Semitism, and most of all, the loss of a mother.

Some days after the lecture was over, I received in the mail a whole bunch of letters from these kids expressing even more strongly how important the experience was for them, just as it was important for me. So I was stimulated by the thought that I would like people to know not only about me, but also about a whole world which disappeared in smoke.

And now I am stimulated anew to write for another reason. I have gotten even more letters, and discovered more interest in my story since *Joe's Violin* came out in 2016, which has convinced me to add the final, exciting chapters to the earlier memoir.

JOE'S VIOLIN

A Survivor Remembers

Joe's drawing of his house in Ghent, New York.

CHAPTER 1
Early Childhood

I think of my father, my mother, my brothers, and together we seem to be a fragment of a world that has vanished, and perhaps what I am trying to do here is to still keep a trace of that world alive. Later on I may be able to clarify for myself more about why I am recording my life story, but for now, let me start from the beginning.

I was born March 23, 1923, in Warsaw, Poland, to my mother Rachel, or as she was known, Ruchele, and to my father Aaron, or as he was known, Aron Shloime. My father was then around thirty, my mother just over twenty-two. I was their first child. My parents told me that it was a joyous occasion in the family. Although my parents were not religious, nevertheless they celebrated my arrival by having a special party for the first-born boy, "Pidyon-ha-Ben." I was told many times later how I was put on a large plate and valuables were given by the guests as some sort of symbolic redeeming. My parents lived in what was later known as the center of the Warsaw ghetto. No such term was known in 1923.

My parents met a couple of years prior to my birth, in a meeting arranged by my mother's oldest brother, who was a friend of my father's. Both my parents' families were poor Jewish hard-working people and they lived on Gensha Street in Warsaw, almost neighbors. I remember the addresses – 29A and 31 Gensha Street.

As I remember, each of these buildings constituted a separate, self-contained world. They had a huge center square yard, which was accessible from the street through gates which were closed at night, and that yard, paved in cobblestones, had a pump in the center which supplied water to all the inhabitants. The tenement buildings were grouped around that yard, and I believe it was a five-story walkup – something which could be compared to our Old Law tenements in New York City, except that they were dense and huge and, being grouped around the yard, constituted a closed world.

Everyone knew the neighbors and they lived in their dark apartments from generation to generation. They were born there and usually they died there. I vaguely recall my mother's parents living in that building. If I am not mistaken, they lived in the basement.

My maternal grandfather was a poor shoemaker. He had seven sons and one daughter. The apartment was very small, so that the entire family would never eat at the same time. During family gatherings there was not even enough room to sit around. I do have fond memories of my uncles, these seven brothers, two of whom survived the war.

I don't recall my father's parents too well in that setting. I do remember my father's father much later on, since he lived with us after he became a widower. He was a carpenter and also quite poor. My grandfather had two sons, one, my father, and three or four daughters, my aunts. These two families knew each other, although they were not very close. Such families were typical in Warsaw at that time, and not considered especially large. My father, like his father, was also a carpenter/wood turner, and this led him to develop a certain specialty. He made wooden heels for women's shoes. I recall seeing my father sitting astride a special bench and whittling out the wooden heel, using a special two-handled knife (an antique tool now seen in country fairs). That street, that location, also evokes memories. Our apartment was behind the front workshop, with a door leading to the street.

Juzio (Joseph) with his parents, at two years old, and Alex, 10 months old.

One time (it was 1926) political demonstrators marched on the street, and mounted police waved sabers. Things took a violent turn, causing my parents to close the store gates. I peeked through a crack in the gate to see the exciting happenings outside. To my horror, I saw the policemen start to hit the demonstrators with their long sabers. It was a frightening experience.

We moved a couple of years later to another apartment, in an industrial section of town on Ogrodowa Street, where again we lived in an industrial building where my father had a larger workshop; in fact, we called it a "fabrica" – factory.

He now had more people working for him. That section of town, called Karcelak, was next to a farmer's market and was a very fascinating world to me. There was a flea market and the variety, noise, unfamiliar faces and lost pennies which we children liked to find after the market was over – was a lot of fun to us.

We lived on Ogrodowa Street until 1933 when we moved out of Warsaw and re-settled in Kielce, a smaller town, more country-like.

I would like to describe our families, or to use a modern term, the extended families, in the midst of which my brothers and I grew up. Alex, or as we called him, Olesh, was born September 25, 1924, and Henry, who was known as Heniush, was born on June 29, 1929. I do remember meeting both my father's and my mother's family frequently, especially on various holidays and for family occasions.

Joseph (far right), Alex, and Henryk, with their parents.

CHAPTER 2
My Mother's Family

My mother, the only girl in the family, had many brothers, two or three who were younger than her. As I remember them, each reflects a different aspect of my childhood and a world vanished. Perhaps writing about them is a way to reconcile such tremendous loss of people and a way of life.

The oldest one was Harzke. It was through him that my father met my mother; they were friends. Harzke was a tailor of children's clothing. He had a marvelous voice, a basso. In fact, the entire family was very much involved in music, particularly in singing. They were too poor to purchase any instruments, but they all had marvelous ears and a great love of music. Harzke was so good that he became an important soloist in the community choir. I was told that once an impresario came over from the U. S. and offered him a job in the States promising him a brilliant singing career. Promises like that were very tempting, but then the busy season in tailoring arrived and the need to support a wife and several children pushed away the dreams of becoming another Koussevitzki (or was it Moishe Oysher?). Harzke, a bear of a man, had a way of stilling my baby cries with his exuberant singing and even managed to make me stop crying and join him in song.

The next brother, Mendel, obviously grew up in the shadow of Harzke and worked with him. Then there was Herschel. He had more ambitious aspirations and, in fact, went to Paris where he learned to become a fashionable barber. Obviously, there was more to it, he could have been a barber in Warsaw without going to Paris. Perhaps he studied modern hair styling for women. The truth of the matter is that, when he came back, he set up a men's barbershop; his youngest brother Yankele (Yacov) worked with him. It was in their barbershop that I had my hair cut.

I do remember this barbershop with great nostalgia. First, the fragrance of the eau-de-Cologne was pervasive; then there were the newspapers, which were attached to sticks so that a customer could sit in a chair, get a shave and a haircut, and at the same time read the paper. But once again music pervades this memory. Both Herschel and Yankel played the mandolin and sang, talked about music, and discussed the accomplishments of the cantor during the last Friday night's service with as much fascination as they would discuss a tenor's performance in the Warsaw Opera (which they also did). They were great opera lovers and conveyed this love of opera to my mother, who in turn conveyed it to her children. Herschel was a good looking man and I admired him for his social polish and his fluency in French.

Another brother, Yossel or Joe, was of a different cut altogether. As I remember him he was rather bald and had what I would call today an apoplectic countenance, with inflamed cheeks. He used to get into fights with people, even with his wife, and it was only our mother who could mollify him, or at least in whose presence he found solace. I remember how on at least one, if not two, occasions, he came to visit us in Kielce, both visits a result of a fight he had with his wife. I was a little bit afraid of him. I didn't trust his quick temper.

Moishe, a fourth brother, was also a man of quick temper, but also of great kindness. I have a vague recollection of going to his wedding. I must have been five, if not younger, and the reason I remember the wedding is something I saw as I wandered the rooms of the place where the reception was taking place. I came across a painting on a wall that frightened me.

In retrospect, I know it depicted Daniel in the pit with the lion, but it was a frightening experience, and it was very often the subject of nightmares which I had later on.

Moishe was a peddler, an unlicensed one, because I remember how his enemy number one was the police – he constantly had to run in fear of being arrested. Nevertheless, he was a man of great kindness and love for his wife Marilyn and his little daughter.

The most fascinating brother of all was Zigmund, again a character so different from all the others. Tall and handsome, he grew up deciding early on that he would get by in life on his charm alone. As poor as he was (as the entire family was), he was a great dresser. A story was told in the family how, in his late teens, he used to dress up on a Saturday morning, get out on the street with a cane and a ring on his finger, and with a nonchalant, imperious gesture, summon a carriage to turn around and pick him up. Obviously, the family admired this, but at the same time, they were a little bit ashamed of him.

He was really a "luftmensch" as it was called. No trade, no binding interests, no family, and, needless to say, no religion. He was a great dancer and he made dancing his profession. The family used to whisper in great shame that he was a "floor dancer." It was later on that I understood what that meant. He was a floor dancer, which meant that he supplied dancing services (and others?) in some nightclubs to some lonely women. Not a very respectable profession, but fascinating nevertheless, especially to me and to my brother. In fact, his very name Zigmund, is also pretentious. It is a Polish name. His Jewish name was Zelig, but Zelig was not going to be known as Zelig. He had to be Zigmund. I remember how he once came to visit us when we lived in Kielce; he was on leave from the Polish army, where he was a member of the cavalry, which was very unusual for a Jew. You had to have a certain height and bearing and he had that, and here he came to visit us with that long coat and a saber all the way down to the floor. I couldn't admire him more.

Yakov, the second survivor of the holocaust, was quite young when I got to know him. I remember him as small of stature, with a broken nose which he got while a member of a boxing team in an athletic club. He got married quite young. I do remember that the entire family (except mother) was against his marrying Alisa simply because he was too young, but he just went ahead and got married.

I remember him very fondly. In 1937 or 1938, when we lived in Kielce, my parents allowed me for the first time to travel to Warsaw by myself during my winter school recess. There I stayed with Yakov and his young wife. No sooner did I arrive, when I got the flu, and I stayed most of my vacation time in bed. We all were very unhappy about it, but several days before the end of my vacation, I got sufficiently well so that Yakov took me to my first opera ever, to the Warsaw Opera House. The opera was *Faust*. It was great excitement for me to get there. Yakov bought the cheapest tickets possible, obviously in the top balcony, and then bribed the usher to let us sit somewhere in a better location.

The production was a daring, modern one, since I remember how they rigged up a loud speaker system in the ceiling of the opera house so that when Mephistopheles's voice comes to taunt Faust, he is not seen, but his voice emanates from a red light in the middle of the ceiling. Very fascinating. The second exciting experience was going to my first symphony concert of the Warsaw Philharmonic. Naturally, we didn't buy tickets, but my family had a friend who worked for a Jewish newspaper and somehow arranged a reporter's pass for me. I was determined at all costs to restrain my constant coughing. I remember the program quite well – it was Grieg's Peer Gynt Suite and his piano concerto. These two experiences, needless to say, left an indelible impression on me. Even now I recall every moment very vividly.

However, as I mentioned, credit for the love of music goes to our mother, with her lovely voice, a good musical ear, and a good musical memory. Most of the music that she knew was taught to her by her friends and her brothers, so she knew numerous arias from operas using Polish words, and she sang them to us. To reciprocate, whenever we were taught a new song in school, it was always with great pleasure that I went back home and taught it to my mother.

After my parents bought violins for Alex and myself, they engaged a violin teacher in Warsaw. I don't think our education went very far, but my interest in the violin persists up to the present and may explain why years later, without hesitation, I purchased the violin in the DP Camp, preferring the warmth of music to that of a coat.

I have a very faint memory of my mother's father and mother. Grandfather was tall and thin. I was told he had a good voice and thus assisted with the services at the synagogue. I don't recall much of my grandmother. They both died when I was quite young, first grandfather, while we were still in Warsaw, and a couple of years later, grandmother.

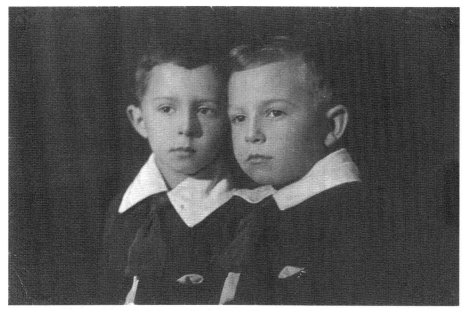

Joseph and his brother Alex, young boys.

CHAPTER 3

My Father's Family

My father's family was also large, though not as large as my mother's. He had one brother, Yossel, and three sisters. I didn't have much contact with Yossel. I know that he was taken to the army, after which he married a woman named Chancia. They had children, with whom we became quite close much later. My father's sister Regina, known as Reggie, was fated to play a large role in our lives in later years. She married Meyer Silverstein at the time that I was born, and they emigrated to the United States. Our family and Reggie's family maintained contact all the way to the beginning of the war. Luckily, it was to them that we finally went after the war, and we became very close.

I recall another aunt, Chaya Feiga, very well. I believe she was the oldest, but remained an old maid. We all knew that she was somewhat eccentric, peculiar. Up to the present time I really don't know what was wrong with her; she was very fond of us children and she lived with her other sister, helping her around the house. We do remember humorous stories that dealt with her mispronunciation of Polish names. Incidentally, both families used Yiddish predominantly. To use Polish was a great effort. The accents were atrocious. None of these people, my uncles and aunts, had any formal education. My uncles, obviously, went to Cheder, which was a religious school where the children were given some very basic primitive knowledge of the Torah. They probably could sign their names in Polish, but I don't think their knowledge of the language went beyond that. This, of course, reflected a reaction to the utter anti-Semitism and contempt that these Jews experienced from the Polish population. As a result, we Polish Jews and, in particular, the lower-class Jews, simply decided for the sake of self-preservation, not to even try to pass or to be exact in cultivating "their" language.

Of course, there was one great exception, Sigmund. That reminds me also of the fact that my father's Polish, as compared to my mother's, was also quite bad. My mother was the educated one, and the best-educated of the whole lot. She finished elementary school and then was sent by her parents to high school, since she was the only girl and, naturally, there was no need to teach her a trade. All the subjects were taught in Russian. She also knew Polish quite well, so as a fruit of her education she could speak Russian, Polish, and Yiddish quite fluently. In fact, with a good musical ear she picked up languages quite easily, and I remember how she studied French later on in the group, as well as Esperanto, that universal language which was devised, if that is the word, by Dr. Zemenhof.

As little educated as my parents were in a formal sense, they, in the manner of a typical striving Jewish family, knew the value of an education, and obviously decided to give their children the best education possible within their means, or maybe even beyond. So when I was old enough (perhaps five years old), they sent me to a kindergarten, a revolutionary idea at that time. This kindergarten was known as the "Freblowka." Many years later, I discovered what Freblowka meant. It was a kindergarten run by the Jewish Socialists along the theoretical lines worked out by Dr. Froehel, a Swiss child psychologist.

CHAPTER 4

Early Schooling

These were my happy days, happy years, because having "graduated" from Freblowka, I was enrolled in a "Cisho" school. That was one of several "veltliche" (non-religious, secular) schools set up by Jewish Socialist parties in Poland. The children were instilled with socialist idealism. All the subjects were taught in Yiddish, but we also had Polish as a language, almost like a foreign language. I spent three years in that school on Krochmalna Street, and those were the happiest years of my childhood. The entire school, looking back, was one big, happy, friendly family. The children were encouraged in all their pursuits, artistic or scientific.

I had two overwhelming interests: the first one was girls. As young as I was, I was a precocious boy; I was madly in love with girls; sometimes one, sometimes two at one time; and then music. Since the school knew about my real love of music, they let me conduct the school chorus. I remember participating in a school play in the role of Father Frost, who was the local version of St. Nicholas, and I sang a song, the melody of which still lingers in my mind.

My great love at that time was a girl named Mirele Potocka, and with her I experienced the first pangs or love (as turned out, unrequited), and jealousy and longing. All this at the ripe old age of seven or eight, or perhaps nine. It was when I was nine that we moved to Kielce. I recall two further happenings in my life which, perhaps in retrospect, influenced me greatly in developing other interests. I remember once being taken to some sort of a celebration, or perhaps it was a performance, and there, far down on the stage was a young girl dancing, dressed in a white filigree dancer's costume, and I was overwhelmed with that world of fantasy, beauty and charm. This little figure bathed in a spotlight dancing on a stage remained in my memory.

Another incident which I also remember quite vividly was when I was taken to a memorial meeting after the death of a Jewish Socialist Bundist leader, Beinish Michalewicz. What caught my attention and then engendered many attempts to recreate it, was a bust of this man on a stage, my first experience of sculpture. I recall that from then on, my favorite pastime, done in great privacy, was to chisel the human profile in the masonry corner of a big brick wall in the factory in Warsaw. I also recall similar attempts in wet sand on the ground. I don't recall being noticed doing any of this. I don't think it would have made much of a difference in my development, but these things are quite vivid in my memory. I remember that my childhood was full of stimuli of one sort or another.

One of the strongest, strangely enough, was politics. My father was an ardent socialist, and belonged to the Jewish Labor Bund. He was quite active. My mother, although not active, was also involved in the political life, and as I understood it later, somewhat to the left of my father. Perhaps, the Russian culture which she acquired in school also gave birth to sympathies for everything Russian, including Russian Communism. Of course, we had no way of knowing, as most of the people didn't, the real situation in Russia. But what we did know was that this was a country where the working man was free, where capitalism was liquidated, and in one word – it was the country of the future of mankind. These were the thirties, a time of the popular front in France, with Leon Blum, the Prime Minister, with the Communists participating, the time of the uprising of the Socialists against Schuschnig's regime in Austria, and finally, the time of the civil war in Spain. We all, and I mean me too, read the daily papers, listened to the radio, and knew the up-to-date situation at the front. We were all very involved. It was with great pride that we gave a sort of sanctuary to my father's cousin, a Communist, who was just released from detention in Lodz with some admonition by the authorities not to engage in any political activity. He came in a clandestine way to us in Kielce, and from us he went to Spain to fight on the Loyalist side. Soon after his arrival there, he was killed on the front.

I considered myself a Bundist like my father, and when we moved to Kielce, I found myself in an utter minority compared to all my friends. Nevertheless, I remember being constantly engaged in very heated political discussions. At that time, discussions and arguments were with the Zionists. I remembered quite well that, with the help of the lessons which I learned by reading the daily Jewish socialist newspaper, the Folkszeitung, I successfully argued that the future of the Jews in Poland was to be found in a socialist Poland; to strive for a Jewish land somewhere else (Uganda or Madagascar were mentioned) was utopian, nationalistic, and contrary to the real interests of the Jews. Their future lay in a socialist system which would do away with anti-Semitism and the exploitation of man by man and thus, do away with a need for a separate state.

In 1932, in the midst of the depression, which affected Poland as much as the rest of the world, my father, searching for economic survival, decided to try his luck in Kielce, a small town south of Warsaw, which was then a center of manufacturing of women's shoes. He first went there by himself. He sold his business in Warsaw and became a partner with some other people in an ongoing business, a large modern factory equipped with automatic machines, which manufactured wooden heels for women's shoes. In 1933, a year later, he brought us to Kielce. Sometime later still, he also brought his brother Yossl, with his family, who became his partner in that business.

My time spent debating the finer points of politics, Socialism, Zionism, and anti-Semitism, were of some use in my quest to survive years later, in ways I couldn't have imagined. For now, Kielce held the promise of livelihood. Schooling was another story.

CHAPTER 5
Moving to Kielce

It was a traumatic experience for me, to give up the warmth, the happiness of that Yiddish school on Krochmalna Street and get enrolled in an elementary public school in Kielce. It was an enormous school with large classes jammed with forty or fifty kids. The school was on Alexander Street, and the kids were mostly Polish with a sprinkling of poor Jewish kids. In the meantime, my father found an apartment in the suburbs of town in a peasant's house, so that the school was within walking distance. It was a typical school for that time and for that place—extremely overcrowded with very harsh discipline, with each class (after some outdoor gymnastics) starting with a Catholic prayer.

Most of the teachers were anti-Semitic, nothing unusual about that, engaging in corporal punishment for mistakes and errors, slapping the hand with a ruler. I remember having a Jewish classmate, his name was Leib. The teacher delighted in taunting him with the name Leibush by also adding Trotsky. "Ah, Leibele Trotsky, come here Leibele, tell us what you know," saying all this with a mock-Jewish accent. All the Polish kids laughed with glee and the Jewish kids were petrified. In spite of or maybe because of all this, my mother took a very active interest in our well-being in this school, and she saw to it that she became a member of the parents' group, Polish parents, mind you. She probably was the only Jewish woman, and became friends not only with the director of the school, but also with the school priest, whose authority was quite great, if not greater than the director's. As a result, the teachers would not dare to touch Alex, Henio or me.

In fact, since we were very good students, my mother persuaded the school's director to consider me along with a handful of other sixth graders, to apply to a Polish high school (gymnasium). Looking back, I must admire my mother's audacity – chutzpah. That high school, Sniadecki's, was absolutely Judenrein, to use a German expression from later years. The last time a Jew was admitted to that school may have been in the nineteenth century. In order to be accepted by the school, the applicants had to pass a very rigorous exam. It was a sensation in town, almost a Jewish holiday, when the results of the exam were published and I passed it.

I was the first Jew in generations to be admitted to the Sniadecki gymnasium. In fact, my admission opened the door to others; my brother Alex was admitted the following year along with several other Jewish kids. We lived in a turbulent sea of anti-Semitism, of a deepening depression, of Hitler coming to power in Germany in 1933, of the Polish government becoming more and more reactionary, and in the midst of all this, this event happened. I was very proud, but at the same time felt a great burden on my shoulders. I must say that I was very much encouraged by my family.

Studying came very easily to me, in spite of anti-Semitic taunting from some of the classmates. I remember one in particular, a member of a minor nobility. When once I dared to say something quite innocent to him, he looked at me with contempt and said, "I don't recall that we were ever tending swine together," or words to that effect. That finished my any attempt to make Polish friends, although I did make friends of a sort with some Polish classmates—Janiczak, Szewczek, Swidor. I remember Swidor in particular. His father was a detective in the police, a plainclothesman. My father was quite active as a Bundist, and we had, every Thursday night, gatherings of friends in our house. This friend Swidor told me in great secrecy that his father's duty was to stand on the corner of the street and take notes on whoever was coming to our house.

Ah yes, those Thursday night gatherings. I was very eager to be a part of these in spite of my youth. I found everything that was going on of great interest and stimulation. The political discussions, the exchange of information of what was going on in Spain, my mother's comments about how she was progressing in Esperanto, and then, the crowning event – my mother's singing of Yiddish folk songs. I recall being asked to take out my violin on a couple of occasions and play something for the guests, in spite of my great shyness.

The truth of the matter was I didn't like the sound which I managed to produce on the violin. That screechy sound was not pleasant even to my ears. Obviously, my parents and the guests didn't think that way.

A great event in those years was the building of our own house. What made this possible was my father's winning a small sum in the Polish state lottery. This enabled him to think seriously about constructing our own house. My mother was sent to the annual trade fair in Poznan. She came back with the plan of an American-style house, which was featured at that fair. It was an unusual house for Poland. It had horizontal wood siding, a flat roof, and picture windows, huge windows. We engaged the services of the local architect, Arnold Kroch, who not only prepared the construction drawings for the house, but upon completion (this was a large house), he and his family occupied one-half of it.

Obviously it was meant to be a two-family house. The house was built on the very outskirts of town, another unusual feature for a Jew in Kielce. I recall every stage of its construction, and I remember quite well the finished house. In fact, I kept drawing it in perspective as a child, over and over and over again at that time, and later on when we had to sell it, and much later when I found myself in Siberia. Drawing this house again and again so lovingly became a tie to my past, and possibly even to my future as an architect.

My father's business did not prosper, and after living in this dream house for two or three years, we had to sell it, and bought an apartment on the main street in town. We lived in that apartment until the outbreak of the Second World War. The times leading up to the outbreak of the war were turbulent in Poland, as they were in the rest of the world.

The Fajngold family at home, before the War, in Kielce, Poland.

CHAPTER 6

Leading up to the War

Personally, I was aware of the fact that although both Alex and I were among those lucky ones who were given a secondary education, our future looked bleak. The newspapers were full of stories about how those few Jewish students who managed to get admitted to the Polish universities were persecuted and required to sit in separate ghetto seats. Also, there was talk about a quota system for the Jewish students, and so many other manifestations of continuously growing anti-Semitism. The Polish authorities made friends with Hitler at that time, and they were apeing his most obnoxious methods of making the lives of Jews miserable. It was with great shame, I remember, when Poland joined Hitler in partitioning of Czechoslovakia, and when Hitler, after having swallowed Austria and other areas, turned towards Czechoslovakia (one of the freedom-loving countries), and demanded and got the Sudetan area inhabited by ethnic Germans. This, I believe, was at the beginning of 1939. Well, there is no point for me to record the entire history, and I must tell about my own personal experiences.

Hitler, having swallowed Czechoslovakia, turned against his "friend" Poland and demanded Gdansk (it was known as Danzig) and the return of the "Polish Corridor." By then, Poland remembered that it was aligned with the Western powers, France in particular. They had a French treaty of mutual help, and Poland, obviously, in cooperation with France and England, refused Hitler's demands.

There was a tremendous amount of hoopla at that time. I recall listening to the speech of the Polish foreign minister, Joseph Beck, which was broadcast every place, and I heard it in our school. Beck ridiculed Hitler's demand of a piece of Polish territory and said that "we can take care of ourselves, we will not succumb the way Czechoslovakia did." Well, of course, it was too late. There was absolutely nothing behind his braggadocio, and, as we all know on September 1, 1939, Hitler's army crossed the Polish border and swiftly started moving east.

A day later, when I was on the balcony of our apartment, we heard the roar of airplane engines. Suddenly, three German planes appeared and dropped a bomb across the street. I was holding a butter dish in my hand and that dish shattered. This was my first experience of the war. I don't think that the bomb did much damage. Nevertheless, a panic set in. As we found out later on, the Polish army crumbled under the onslaught of Hitler's Panzers.

An official announcement was made telling the male population they must leave the town and run east toward the Vistula River and cross it, because there the Polish army would put up a resistance and defeat the Germans. The panic must have affected many people. So on September 3, with the Germans nowhere in sight yet, my father took Alex and me and with some friends, we simply started running east, leaving our mother and youngest brother Henry behind. The panic must have been great for my father, who undoubtedly loved his family, to leave them like that, but he was one of many thousands who did that. At that time, we did not just run from the German army, because we hardly knew what was in store for us as Jews – nobody knew. It was supposed to be on orders from higher Polish authorities for the male population to run and create some kind of resistance further east.

CHAPTER 7
Outbreak of War, 1939

We were hardly several kilometers outside of town when German fighter planes appeared. There was absolutely no resistance, no anti-aircraft fire of any sort, nor were there any Polish planes to appear and engage in any dogfights with the German planes. These planes came very low over the column of thousands of people crowding the road going east, and started shooting at us with their machine guns. All the people scattered into the roadside ditches, into the fields, and we stayed down until the planes disappeared. We then continued our flight east.

Several hours later, again the planes appeared. We decided it was dangerous to flee in broad daylight. We found a refuge in some shed during the day. When darkness fell, we continued our flight. My father's objective was to reach his birthplace, a very small town, a shtetl called Zawichost, which was on the Vistula River. We continued walking east all night long. Of course, we did not make Zawichost that night; we had to stop at daybreak, but since there were no visible German planes, we continued going. I got blisters on my feet; walking was very painful, but we had to go. My father carried us, a little bit me, a little bit Alex, and we kept on going further and further east.

Suddenly, the next day German planes appeared again. We ran for cover under a tree. The Germans saw us running and started shooting at us with machine guns. Luckily, we were not hit, but a whole shower of leaves fell on our heads and backs. The following day, we finally came to Zawichost. We quickly reached father's relatives' house. As it turned out, most or all of the people had abandoned the town We could not find anyone. My father found an old Polish peasant who operated some sort of makeshift ferry, and took us across the Vistula River to the eastern shore. As we were crossing the river at night, we saw on the horizon the sky all lit up. It was the wooden bridge in Sandomierz burning, having been bombed by German planes. My father had some memories of that bridge. In the First World War the previous bridge had been destroyed. The Russians, at that time in control of the area, mobilized all the able-bodied people to reconstruct the bridge, and my father was among them, as was his father too. That same bridge lasted until that very night when we were crossing the Vistula River some 10 or 15 kilometers further north.

Now the object of our flight was a little town further east, not quite on the shore of the Vistula River, named Zaklikow. My father had some relatives there. Zakikow in some miraculous way, had remained an island of tranquility completely untouched by these momentous cataclysms around it. We found my father's relative, a cousin, her husband and a child, but before we could settle we had to register with the local authorities as though there were no war, no chaos, no panic, everything the way it was supposed to be.

We were received by our relatives, fed, made comfortable, and were at a loss to know what to do next. They listened to the tale of our flight with great apprehension, scared about what life was about to bring them. I do not remember if it was at that time, or a couple of days later, when we found out that the German army during that blitzkrieg managed to bypass this little insignificant town and were already in control of the entire hinterland. They took Lublin, a town further east, almost by the river Bug.

Towards the evening, we suddenly heard the tremendous roar of planes. We ran out and started counting. There were probably about twenty-four bombers. I believe these black monsters were Stukkas. They flew very low over that little town and the next thing we heard were explosions of bombs. In great panic, all of us ran into the house and its cellar, and closed the doors and the trap door over the ladder to the cellar. There we experienced what seemed to us an endless hell of explosions shaking the foundations of that dark, dank cellar. Everybody was mortally frightened. Suddenly, we started smelling smoke. We assumed that the house was on fire, but the acrid smells may also have been detonated gas.

Let's not forget that this was the beginning of the war and we had no way of knowing if the Germans were going to use poison gas. We didn't know what to do first. Everyone grabbed some piece of clothing and wet it in water someplace, and put it on their faces. This we thought might save us from poison gas, but when we looked outside, we saw that the houses across the street were in flames. Not this house – miraculously. We ran out and saw that the entire little town was in flames. We somehow managed to find a way on the street between the burning houses and ran out to the outskirts up on a hill, where we spent the rest of the day and the entire night just watching the town being turned into cinders.

I cannot forget one scene as we were abandoning this house. My father's cousin and his wife were a young couple with a child, and obviously they took great pride in the way they fixed up their house. The wife was especially proud of the new handmade lace curtains. So in this great panic when we had to run for our lives, she decided that she must save these curtains. We all had to drag her away into the safety of the open space. As I said, we spent the rest of the day and the entire night, and perhaps the following day outside, just helplessly sitting there and watching, and when the flames died down we went down into what remained in the smoldering town in search of food. The only food we found were wafers from a burned-out ice cream stand. We remained in town a short time longer, but there was no place to stay. We heard from other survivors that the entire countryside and, in fact, whatever remained of Poland outside of the areas which were at the same time occupied by the Russian army on

September 17, was already occupied by the Germans. We then decided to turn back and return to Kielce.

It just so happens that in the last couple of weeks my memory of this experience came vividly back to me in connection with the 40th anniversary of the destruction of Dresden. I could not, and I still cannot, find in me the capacity to shed tears over the destruction of Dresden. In fact, it is an affront to the memories of people who died to shed tears over that beautiful city, which was destroyed in 1945.

When the Germans dropped their first bombs in Kielce in 1939, in the middle of the town, there was absolutely not a single military object or target. The German planes shot at us with machine guns on the road. We were helpless refugees, civilians – not a military unit which they wanted to kill, and that liitle town Zaklikow was definitely not a military object. I know from history what happened to Rotterdam, to Coventry, but that was later. These were the first two weeks of the Second World War, when the German planes completely destroyed, firebombed, a small, helpless village. It was not a beautiful town. It had no memorials to the splendor of the German court, to baroque architecture, etc., so it wasn't worth mentioning. I, however, cannot forget it. The world should not fall for these distorted, unjustified feelings of guilt.

Our return back to Kielce was uneventful. The entire countryside was occupied by the German army, but they were busy manning the Eastern border, and there were not many Germans to be seen on the roads. We made our trip back to Kielce in just a couple of days. We rejoined our family, our mother and youngest brother, who were still in our apartment.

Soon, within days, there was a shortage of bread. Long lines of people stood in front of the bread stores. However, no Jews were allowed to stand on these lines. They were simply kicked out. I am not sure if the Poles were instrumental in kicking out the Jews, but there were always

German soldiers constantly shouting, "Jude Raus." Here, my Aryan, Polish appearance came in very handy. I had Aryan features and the Poles, having lived with the Jews for so many generations, could distinguish a Jew by imperceptible, minute signs like the shape of the head, or the hairline in the back, besides of course, the Jewish accent. Both in looks and in speech I could pass without any difficulty as a Pole. So it was my duty to stand in these lines for bread and other food items, which helped my family stay out of hunger.

Soon, other discriminatory rulings and edicts appeared. The Germans decided to hold 10 prominent Jews as hostages for two weeks, after which they would be replaced by other hostages. The idea was that if there was no harm done to any German soldiers occupying our town, the hostages would be released; otherwise, they would be shot.

Our father was one of the first hostages to serve. I remember how we all felt about his safety. Not being religious, we did not pray. We just hoped fervently that he would be released unharmed. These were the longest two weeks, and he was finally released. In the meantime, all the Jews were organized in brigades and were given some meaningless tasks to perform. Jews who were dressed in the traditional Jewish *capotas* and caps were especially mistreated. Their beards were shorn. They were beaten up and made fun of. This was done by the Germans, but the Poles were gleefully looked on with pleasure.

Not long after my father was released, he was called in to the Gestapo, the German secret police. He was kept several days, as I remember, where they interrogated him about his activities and about the Jewish Socialist Party. All of us were extremely worried. Rumors were circulating; news of what was happening in other towns managed to drift in, and it was the consensus of opinion of my parents' friends that if and when he was released from his first interrogation, he must immediately disappear, because, as we were told, it is the German policy to re-arrest the suspect soon after the initial release, and send him to a concentration camp.

The only concentration camps we knew of at that time were Dachau in Germany, and another new Polish camp which was set up by the Poles themselves before the war. When, finally, my father was released, he did not go back to our home, but instead he was taken in by a friend who had a house somewhere in the suburbs. This friend arranged to hire a horse and an open buggy to take my father to safety. At that point, my parents decided that, perhaps, the best thing would be if I would take this opportunity and go with father to the Russian-occupied part of Poland where, we were told, the Polish schools, especially high schools, were re-opened, although run by the Russians.

Compared to what we had just witnessed in Kielce and around, Communist Russia would be a place of freedom.

CHAPTER 8
Going to Lvov, December 1939

My parents thought so highly of the need for education that they couldn't bear my loss of further schooling. So the following morning my father and I and a friend of his who was also active in the Bund, arranged ourselves in the hay on that buggy, and after we said goodbye to my mother, we started east. As we started moving, I turned my head and saw my mother's tear-streaked face. Suddenly at this moment I became aware of the enormous significance of this act of leaving my mother. And the thought came to me: will I see her again? This image of my lovely mother waving to us, in tears, came to haunt me again and again in the years to come. Yes my guilt, my enormous guilt!

I do not remember all the details of our travel east. But after several days of travelling the bumpy roads of the Polish countryside, we crossed the Vistula River and went on further east, until we reached the town of Lublin. At that time, the situation was as follows: Poland all the way from the Western border to the River Bug was occupied by the German Army. The Russians, by prior arrangement, occupied the eastern part of Poland, and their army faced the Germans on the Bug River. Of course, they were not enemies, but allies. Those who remember their history know that the so-called Ribentroff-Molotov pact was at first a non-aggression pact, where they worked out the manner in which they would divide Poland, and that pact was soon supplemented by a friendship pact between

Communist Russia and Nazi Germany. Lublin was occupied by the Germans. We entered the town, and I remember distinctly how I came across some German soldiers, with whom I engaged in a discussion about the future and how they told me, "Ah yes, next we will conquer Russia."

In Lublin my father managed to get in touch with a Polish guide, a peasant, who promised for a fee to take us through the woods and across the border into Russian-occupied Eastern territory. The following night we were on our way. We walked for miles in the pitch blackness of the cloudy night, stumbling upon trees and ditches. Finally, the guide stopped and said, "Here we are, all you have to do now is to cross a small stream in front of you," which by the way we did not see, it was that dark. He was paid and disappeared. Our group that was attempting to cross the border consisted of about eight people or so; besides my father and a friend of his, and some other grownups, there were three or four other youths and myself. We couldn't see the stream in the darkness, so we found long sticks and grappled with them in front of us as we walked until we finally came across that stream. As it turned out, it was deep in some places and shallow in other places, but we had no way of discovering the best place for fording the water. We couldn't afford to waste more time, so we finally crossed that stream submerged up to our stomachs in this icy water. The date was December 1, 1939. We went some kilometers past the stream, as we just hoped that we were going in the right direction, since we had no guide of any sort, no light.

Suddenly we saw a flicker of light. The light came closer and closer, but quietly. It was a ghost-like experience. Then the light disappeared. We kept on stumbling in the darkness toward some apparition in the distance, which may have been a little village. Suddenly, we heard rough voices. Two young peasants were upon us holding a flashlight, and one of them (at least one if not the other) had a gun, and demanded from us yids (Jews) all our valuables. I remember how the youths in our group whispered, should they jump them, but my father was afraid that we would be overpowered, especially since they were armed. So we gave them all the valuables we had, whatever we had, watches, some money. They quickly took it and disappeared.. We were cold and wet and frightened and intent on going, and finally we came to a clearing and railroad tracks. We followed these tracks (by then it was daylight), which led us to a station, and we realized by some signs that we were on the Russian-occupied side. We were safe.

What followed was my first experience of seeing and talking to Russians. When a train came, we entered a car and there, in a crowded compartment, we came across some Russian soldiers. They were very friendly to us. They greeted us, exchanged friendly banter, and somehow with my Polish and a certain amount of German, I managed to exchange some greetings with them. During that exchange, I found out that one of these Russians was not a plain soldier, but a man of a certain military rank. I was quite impressed with their friendliness. It was a friendliness which I experienced in the following years over and over again.

We soon arrived in the main Polish town of that Eastern territory occupied by the Russians, namely Lvov. The Soviets, in occupying the eastern part of Poland, used the fact that the indigenous rural population of that area was predominantly Ukrainian to claim that what they did was liberate this territory from the Polish "Panys." They then promptly incorporated it into the Ukraine. The northerly part was likewise incorporated into Byelorussia. Then we reached Lvov, and we got in touch with some people that my father knew about, who had come to Lvov previously and who helped us to get established.

What that meant for me was that I had to find a functioning high school where the teaching language would still be Polish, as well as finding some accommodations. I was successful in finding both. The Russians placed great importance on winning the sympathies of the young, and this they did at this time as well as in the years to come, by providing free education to all as well as living accommodations for the students.

However, my father could not find any work at all. In fact, he did not expect to find any. The town was swollen with millions of refugees, everyone looking for ways to make a living or to survive, to be more exact, and it was his plan to do what others did, that is to get engaged by the Russians as a carpenter in their industry someplace outside of Lvov. We really had no idea whatsoever about the working or living conditions in Russia.

It was the common belief among all these refugees that it was a great privilege to be given work in this land of the proletariat. I remember a friend of my father's, a Communist no less, was refused working papers and a contract because his father was a merchant and not a proletarian. Besides, being a Polish Communist at that time was no recommendation in the eyes of the Russians. It seems that the Polish Communists were disgraced even before the war by the Komitern, because obviously they didn't know to align themselves with the winning factions at the time of the bloody purges taking place in the Soviet Union in the mid-thirties. Anyway, my father was "lucky" to be given a contract to do work as a carpenter in the industrial belt of the Ukraine in the Donbass region (the basin of the River Don). He said goodbye to me and left.

I found my schooling and my life in this communal living quarters extremely stimulating. The place was full of very bright young men (and women? I don't recall any!) from all over Poland who came to Lvov expressly for the same purpose that I did. All of them were involved in intense intellectual pursuits. I started studying Russian and read Marxist philosophy. Discussions were going on day and night. Naturally, the predominant political orientation was Communism. I got swept away by this climate. I knew very little about the actual development of Communism in the Soviet Union. Well, no one did. Of course, little did we know how misled the world was about what really was taking place is Russia. We probably believed in the guilt of all these traitors who were murdered by Stalin in the thirties – Zinoviev, Kamyenev, Bucharin, Radek, and Tuhachefsky. We swallowed the argument that when you make an omlet, you have to break some eggs. The Russians with whom we did have contact made a very favorable impression. Brotherhood, idealism, and faith in the future reigned supreme. All this, plus free education. But I was otherwise, cold and miserable, without any adequate funds, and came down with the flu. I wasn't dressed properly, I was underfed. I missed my parents and brothers; sleeping in the cold, unheated rooms and urinating a dozen times in the middle of the night was common. But with all this, it was one of the most stimulating times of my youth.

In the beginning of spring 1940, something disturbing became noticeable. Along with the great number of military trains going back and forth, carrying tanks and artillery pieces (which obviously boded nothing good), people, those lucky chosen who found employment inside Russia, started trickling back. They brought back tales of horrible working and living conditions. In the beginning, we dismissed those tales as those of malcontents, people who are always against Socialism, softies who couldn't really tolerate the rigors of hard but honest work. However, more and more of those people started coming back. It became obvious that a lot of those disillusioned refugees wished to go back to the German-occupied part of Poland to rejoin their families, since they had no information that anything bad was happening to them. The general feeling was that the situation could not be any worse than it was in the Russian-occupied part. In any case, the pull of family ties was very strong, so more and more people registered to rejoin their families. Amidst all this, on a day some time in April or May, my father returned. I greeted him with mixed feelings. I was happy to see him, but I was also disappointed that he was like the other refugees who couldn't tolerate the working conditions. But his tale of what he really found in Russia was convincing enough to show me that he was right. It turned out that they made him a carpenter to build supports inside coal mines. Work was very hard. Food was inadequate, no clothing, no special allowance as we take for granted here in the U.S. There were no real unions of this sort, and, of course, the pay was very low. He felt that he had no choice but to simply turn around, in fact, escape and come back to the unsettled conditions of Lvov. He too decided that was going to take a chance with his life and go back to rejoin his family, his wife, and remaining two sons, my brothers, in Kielce. Our decision then was that I was to remain and enjoy the fruits of my life in Lvov, which I found so much to my liking.

CHAPTER 9

Arrested by Russian Secret Police, May 1940

New rumors started spreading to the effect that the Soviet authorities were going to re-settle all those refugees who were not citizens to the regions deep inside Russia. Since by then we knew what the conditions inside Russia were, there was a panic among those refugees. We students organized a committee, of which I was a member, and we sent a delegation (I was part of it), to a famous Polish writer, Wanda Wasilewska, who was at that time popular and cooperative with the Soviet authorities; in fact, she married a famous Russian playwright. We thought that she was the person who could help us students, ardent sympathizers, to remain in Lvov, and continue our studies. She assured us that, "Yes indeed, you have nothing to worry about; you will not be resettled."

The rumors about the Russians arresting refugees and resettling them to the deep interior became a fact. Every night thousands of people were picked up, their documents checked, and packed in freight trains and shipped out. We students were afraid that the same would happen to us, so we decided not to sleep in our dormitories, instead we slept in an adjacent park. This life couldn't go on indefinitely. We then sent another delegation to Wasilewska, and again she assured us that nothing was going to happen to us. The day before, my father was picked up along with others, and I started frantically searching for him. I couldn't get any place to find out where he was or where he was being sent. That night most of the students did not sleep in the park anymore, but back in the dormitories, and that night, sure enough, the Russian police came and picked us all up. We were taken to the railroad yards and placed in freight cars. We protested to no avail. When I started demanding to be sent to the same place where my father was, they said, "Sure, sure, don't worry, don't worry."

We got locked up in these freight cars and we remained in them for a considerable time, a day or days. Then the train started moving. The time was June, 1940. After a day of travelling, some place at a small railroad junction, an armed guard opened the doors and let the whole trainload of people out into a field where they set up a kitchen and served us bread and soup. Then, back to the train, they locked the doors again, and the train kept moving; we had no idea where. My particular train car was tightly jammed with people of different ages and backgrounds. There were old and young women, small children, teenagers, old men and five fellow students. In the middle of that car, curtained off with sheets, was a wooden trough. This was supposed to be our toilet. We travelled day and night with frequent stoppings with the doors constantly closed. We lost our time orientation. The armed guards (members or the N.K.V.D., the interior police force, with their dreaded red bands on their caps) would open the doors to let us out to be fed at irregular intervals. After two or three weeks of such travelling, the doors were opened and we were told that from now on, we could travel with the doors open. What a relief! We would then look outside into the countryside and get an orientation of where we were going. After several days, we stopped at a town named Uffa. I remembered from my geography lessons in high school that Uffa was the main town in the Urals region. These mountains separate Europe from Asia. We got out of the train to be fed the usual cabbage soup and porridge and were given a ration of bread. A quick glance showed me that there was a river a short distance away. I quickly jumped into the river, where I washed myself thoroughly. We were soon called to board the train again. Somehow at that time, perhaps being weakened or in a bad emotional state, I lost consciousness. When some people revived me and I was capable of standing on my feet, a Russian woman came over to me and said in Russian, "Don't worry, you will get used to it. And if you don't get used to it you will die like a dog." I remember the Russian expression. This particular expression was to haunt my entire stay in Russia. It is almost like a cliché, saying it applies to everybody. If you cannot get used to the conditions, you will die.

At that time, there were prisoners in these trains. We were underfed and in extremely unsanitary conditions, and yet to my great horror, when we stopped someplace on the railroad siding deep inside Russia, suddenly Russian peasants came running up to us asking us for bread. They were starving. This situation was horrible and made no sense to us. They asked *us* for bread! How was this possible? But they were free! Well, that was the situation, as we found out later, very common for the Russian peasantry under Communism. We boarded the train and kept on moving east, day and night, riding for hours, riding again, stopping, being fed at odd hours in the middle of the night, then an hour later, then not again for 24 hours, then again a little bit. Moving on further and further east on the Trans-Siberian railroad. My knowledge of geography was helpful to me, so I knew where we were as we passed Chelabinsk, Pscov, Novosibirsk, and further east, Irkutsk. After a couple more weeks of this kind of travelling, the train finally stopped and everyone was ordered out with all their belongings, whatever they were. After waiting for some days, the entire trainload of people was packed into open trucks, and we started travelling north on a dirt rugged road. The road was leading straight north through the Taiga, or the pine forest. That trip took well over a week and covered over 800 kilometers. I remember being fed day after day salted herring and, of course, tea. We finally arrived in a small town called Aldan. From there convoys of several trucks each went in different directions. I found myself in a truck convoy that went to a small "settlement" called Chvoyni.

As it turned out, Chvoyni was a small village consisting of about a half dozen log cabins surrounded by the forest. The entire region was called the Yacut autonomous region. It was supposed to be an autonomous land for the indigenous Yacut population, which were of Mongolian appearance. At that time, of course, we did not see any Yacuts. We were all in the charge of officers of the NKVD, the interior police. One officer assigned cabins to a group. Our cabin was assigned to the single men, which meant four young men, my age or so, and three very old and feeble men. Each cabin was approximately 25 by 25 feet square. In the middle was a tin oven with a tin pipe going through the roof. No toilet facilities, no water, no bathroom, nothing. In the other barracks were mostly other older men, women and children. As it turned out, this settlement, one of numerous others, was supposed to be for people who were sent to Siberia to do, comparatively speaking, light work, light labor. We soon found out what that labor was. We were organized in teams, given long hand saws and axes, and we were told to fell trees, and cut them up in different lengths. Some of the pieces were either for further splitting into firewood for the local power station or for the construction of supports in the gold mines of the region. My experience (or anyone else's for that matter), in felling trees was not very extensive.

What about my father? I had no idea where he was sent. My entreaties to the local police officers brought no results whatsoever. In fact, what I did come across was a very cynical attitude on their part, when it came to the question of uniting families. Men separated from women or vice versa were told, "It is not a big deal, you will find someone else and start a new family," or, "Don't worry about your father. We will take good care of him." We were allowed to write, and since this was still the time of peaceful, even friendly relations between Germany and Russia, I managed to send out some letters to my mother and, miracle of miracles, I received some letters back. Included in them were some photographs of my mother and brothers. Incidentally, I did have photographs with me

when I left home and I treasured them like my most precious posses-
sions. From those letters, I found out not only that my mother and my two
brothers were alive, and that Alex was working along with his uncle Joe
and his cousins Shlomo and Leon in our factory (this time, for the German authorities), but also that my mother had received a letter from my
father, who was sent into a hard labor camp deep inside European Russia
in the vicinity of Vitesk. When I received a proper address from her, I sent
a letter to my father. Of course, each letter took a long time, weeks and
week to arrive and then for the reply to come back, more weeks. Thus, I
received a letter from my father too, and this way I found out where he
was, that he was still alive, and working very, very hard.

To digress somewhat, the thought of writing down my memories
of the war years has been with me for quite some time. My father, soon
after coming to the U.S. in 1946, also decided to write down whatever he
remembered of his experience in Russia. He wrote down some reminiscences and sent them to the Yiddish newspaper, *The Forward*. The editors
decided to digest these memoirs and, using some highlights, published
them in the form of a letter to the editor. The other day, while dictating
these reminiscences, I thought of my father's memoirs, and then, going
through some old papers and documents which I saved for close to 40
years, I came across these notes (not the published "letter"). They were
written in Yiddish, a rough draft on note paper in pencil. Starting to read
them, it occurred to me that perhaps at this point, I should incorporate
my own English translation of my father's memoirs here. I realized, however, that for people without the experiences which I had, it is impossible
to recognize the ramifications of the Russian legal system. I feel that I
should, perhaps, insert some clarifying remarks at this point.

CHAPTER 10

My Father Is Taken to a Labor Camp

The Soviet Union had a constitution, which on the face of it is supposed to give various civil rights to the individual. Of course, not to the extent that we have in the U.S., but nevertheless, there are civil rights. In practice, however, and especially under Stalin's regime, the Soviet constitution was continuously violated, and the attitude, which I mentioned before, was quite cynical. People were arrested for the slightest offense, if it was conceived by the authorities to be an offense. Lack of proper enthusiasm, not enough applause, some belittling remark about a Russian leader, anything of that sort was enough to get arrested. The usual procedure was for the prisoner to be sent to jail, interrogated, and then after some months, sometimes longer, to be told that he has been sentenced for counter-revolutionary activities under Section 38 or 39 (it seems the Russians know the sections by heart), to five or seven years of hard labor. Such a prisoner was then sent to one of thousands of labor camps, where all the great achievements of the regime were brought to life—all the big dams, mines, factories, canals, and the opening of new territories, and all the other great achievements that the Soviet regime was proud of, were nothing but products of this kind of labor. Very often people were sent from jail directly to the labor camp, a "Gulag Archipelago," and then a long time after, notified that they had been sentenced. One did not have to be present at the trial. It was enough to be sent to the commandant of the labor camp one day, called from work, and be told that the Troika, as it was called (three judges) found you guilty for counter-revolutionary activities, and you were sentenced. My own history doesn't even have that. I have not been told, as I couldn't have been, that I along with other teenagers and women and children and old people, were found guilty of counter-revolutionary activities.

So, we did light labor as prisoners without being sentenced, but not so with my father. He was sent to a hard labor camp, and there, after months of unbearable conditions, was told of his sentence. Of course there was no trial. The place where my father was sent was called Volgastroi. It was in North Central Russia, not far from a town named Rybinsk. There thousands and thousands of people were building a huge hydroelectric establishment, which involved a huge river dam and buildings for the industrial complex.

The first page of my father's notes seems to start from a certain midpoint. I could not find the description of his travel to the labor camp or anything else that may have happened in the period between June and November 1940.

CHAPTER 11

My Father's Memoirs from the Labor Camp, 1940 to 1942

Here from my father's memoirs, is his own story, in his own words:

We are now in the third section of Volgostroi. It is quiet and sad. We are very affected by the fact that we are to remain slaves in these camps. It's a very cold November night. We arrived at the third section, cold, wet, and hungry. They sent us to the barracks. Here there was a little bit more organization this time, so that each one had his own space in the barracks. These barracks were especially constructed for us prisoners. They were a little bit more spacious than the previous ones. In the march that we had to make, we lost over thirty people who couldn't make it, and they died. Also, some sick people fell by the wayside, so as a result, we have more room. From experience I know, just because we are in a new place doesn't mean that the conditions will be better than the previous camp. We were already experienced prisoners, and we managed to work out some kind of relationship and understanding with the managers. Besides, in the other camp we had several medical commissioners who came to visit us, and we were in such bad conditions that we were ordered to perform only light labor, but even this light labor was too heavy for us, since each one had to fulfill a certain minimum ("norma").

When we were arrested, the great majority of us Polish Jews managed to take with us personal belongings, especially coats, shoes, etc. Every several days the camp authorities conducted searches of our personal belongings, and whenever they saw our personal items or clothing, these Russian officials couldn't get over how well made and beautiful these coats and shirts and shoes were. So they offered us a trade: for a shirt they would give us a week of light work. For a coat, perhaps more, and they would overlook the non-fulfillment of the norma. Or course, those who had nothing to give, did not have this advantage, so those who were better off threw to the less fortunate pieces of bread. All this was in the old camp.

In the new camp, we had to start from scratch. All the findings of the medical commissions which certified when a particular prisoner was too sick to perform heavy work, were not recognized in the new camp, and here the management was not for some reason interested in trading favors for clothing. Every evening as soon as we all finished our soup, there was always a search of all our belongings, and then everyone went to sleep, holding tight to whatever he managed to save. We had to get up between four and five o'clock in the morning. There were washing facilities, but so few that in the very short time allotted for it, only a few people managed to wash up. There were 120 people waiting to get to a sink. If you cared to clean up, you had to get up in the middle of the night to do it. I also want to add that there was no soap. In the morning after we finished our soup, we had to form into new brigades at the gate. Before starting to march out to work, they asked whoever is sick should step out of the line. One day all people stepped out and all were sick. The next day, they did not ask anymore in the morning, but they told us that whoever is sick should go to the polyclinic after work.

The place of work was about two kilometers away. Each one of us received a spade and an axe or a pick iron. Upon arrival at the job site, we had to wait two and a half hours until there was daylight. Then they told us what to do. We were building a tremendous, huge water dam. The bulk of the work, the moving of earth, was done by bulldozers. Our task was to smooth out the grooves which were left by the bulldozer. We had to either add earth, or take away some in order to achieve the proper levels.

Our camp had 2,000 prisoners. Besides us people from Poland, there were about 1500 Soviet citizens. Among those were prisoners who were finishing their term, and there were others who had a certain freedom of movement, and these Soviet prisoners managed to go to the town of Rybinsk, which was just several kilometers away. So this was an opportunity for us to make deals with these Soviet prisoners. The prisoners would go to Rybinsk and bring back some food products. Lucky were those who had things to exchange. The great majority or us had nothing left anymore to exchange, no coats, no pants, no shirts. So the hunger was getting worse and worse.

In the meantime, it was getting colder and colder. The earth was getting frozen and almost impossible to dig. After two or three weeks we couldn't stand any longer on our feet. In the evening when we were permitted, there was a great crowd trying to see the doctor at the clinic. It was only the stronger sick people who managed to force their way in to see the doctor. The weaker ones gave up. Those lucky ones who did see the doctor received just a token of attention. The only thing that the doctor did was to take their temperature and he gave each one of us some liquid to drink, and ordered us in the morning to go to work. It was very rare that anyone was excused from work the next day. The minimum temperature that one had to have in order to be considered for not working was 38 ½ degrees Celsius. In addition, since all work in Russia is measured in "norma," it was obvious that the doctor also had a "norma" for how many people he was allowed to declare sick enough not to work or to be sent to light work.

A man in our brigade couldn't stand anymore, and yet he was not excused by the doctor. In the morning, we all had to leave the barrack and we had to help carry him outside, holding him under his arms, but we couldn't take him outside the gate, so we had to leave him where he fell in the snow. The commandant who saw the incident made no remark. Not only that, he had some prisoners pick him up and throw him outside the gate. In the evening, when we returned to our camp from work, we came across a horse and buggy and on that buggy, on that platform, was the body of the man who died during the day. We saw people dying daily, but this particular incident made an especially depressing effect on me.

Another day, in the evening, we dragged ourselves back to the barracks, to the camp from work, and outside the gate we were met by two Russian guys, vigorous, and they asked us in a cheerful manner, "Finished work?"

"Yes," we said.

"And where is the brigadier [the chief of the brigade]?" They asked us to point out our chief, a prisoner like us. They wanted to check the work, they said. They looked officious enough for us to believe them, so that the brigadier turned around and went with them back to the work site. In the meantime, we dragged ourselves slowly towards the gate and suddenly, after about 20 minutes, we see someone running in just underwear. That was our brigadier. Of course, what these two guys did, is they simply forced him to give up all of his clothing to them, and let us not forget that it was extremely cold at that time. Yes, I remember this man, he was a journalist from Vienna by the name of Beck. When we went to the chief of the camp, he simply laughed at us, and he said, "Write a report if you want to. And besides," he said, "why do you wear such good clothing from Poland? It is your own fault."

In this camp, we so-called political prisoners were mixed in with criminal prisoners, and as a result, we were subject to continuous thievery, beatings and mistreatment. Our hunger was getting worse with every day. In the evening, we were getting our bread portion for the entire day – 300 grams. But it was foolish to leave it any place, so we all ate the bread all at once, which also meant that for the rest of the day we had hunger pangs all day long, and the little soup that we got in the middle of the day didn't help much. So days followed days of feast and famine, 300 grams of bread in the evening, and just water soup the next day. I still had on my Polish suit from home, and I didn't know if I should sell it and get some additional food, or perhaps, they will after all free us. I was getting hungrier every day, so I decided to sell it for 280 rubles. I thought that for the money I would be able to buy some food from these Russian prisoners who had special privileges. I bought one portion of bread, and that was the last portion of bread I got for my money.

Obviously these criminal elements knew that I had money, so the very next day, when I went out to get my soup, two guys fell upon me and they went through all my pockets and they found the money and took it. Of course, I couldn't go to the camp chief and complain because I couldn't admit that I sold the suit, which was illegal. Besides, what happened to me happened to dozens and dozens of my fellow prisoners, Jews from Poland, and of course, their complaints brought no result whatsoever. There were a few fellow prisoners who managed somehow to bring with them and save a lot of belongings, and they had it very good. However, I must say, they didn't give a damn about their fellow prisoners who were literally dying from hunger, and no attempt was made by any one of them to help with a piece of bread.

Some days later, as I was lying there on that narrow board which constituted my bed, a neighbor asked me to lend him the little knife that I had. Of course, it was illegal to have knives, but I found in the woods a piece of a broken saw, and from that piece I fashioned a knife, which was a very useful item. That little knife was constantly being asked for by fellow prisoners. It was a very desirable item, and when I was lying there it occurred to me that perhaps I could sell it, since it was the only thing of value that I had with me.

I was getting weaker and weaker. One morning, as I was trying to go down from bed, I lost consciousness. Somehow the fellow prisoners revived me and helped me outside. I managed somehow to pull myself to the work site, but when they gave me a wheel barrow, where I had to take earth from one place to another, I felt I couldn't do it, especially since I had to go across a narrow plank over a deep pit. Sure enough, as I was trying to negotiate that narrow plank, I lost my balance and I feel into the pit. I thought that was the end of my life. Somehow they dragged me out and I dragged myself to the brigadier and, believing that these were my last days, I beseeched him to remember my name and my family's address, and notify them, when he had a chance, about what happened to me. That evening, which I thought would be my last day, a miracle happened. We were notified that we were ordered to form for brigades, and that these brigades would be sent out to a new location. I knew that any change could only be for the better, because in this third section I could not survive. The next day, they sent us to the second section, and about that I'll write some other time.

This is the end of my father's notes concerning his days in the labor camp. Let me go back to my own story.

CHAPTER 12

My Life in Aldan, Eastern Siberia

As I said before, all single men, teenage boys and older men were put in a separate barracks. All the barracks were log cabins, each with a central stove, but no insulation whatsoever, and needless to say, no elementary provisions for sanitation. Wind blew between cracks of the logs. Little did we realize how ill-prepared we were for the harsh winter to come, and the camp authorities didn't give us any guidance or help to prepare for survival. The time when we finally settled down must have been September, 1940. This part of Siberia, situated in the northeast corner, was probably the coldest inhabited region of the world. I learned in school that the so-called "North Pole of coldness" was a place called Vyerhoyansk, which was within the same region. Sure enough, by the end of September, winter was upon us. Snow started coming down day and night, without interruption. As a result, there were paths connecting the barracks and the outside road with banks fo snow on each side well over four or five feet high. The temperature dropped and eventually it reached minus 60 or 65 degrees Centigrade. We met some "free" Russians (by the way, all the non-Yacut population in that entire region were people who were exiled to this area after serving prison terms),

The people that we came across were very helpful in many ways. They gave us advice as to how to behave in this cold weather, and the first rule was never to go out by oneself. It was important to observe the other person to see if his cheeks or nose were getting frost-bitten, a very common occurrence. Our situation was desperate. We were not given any special warm insulated clothing or felt boots, which were a necessity in this climate. The old timers, the Russians we came across, did have felt boots and cotton insulated coats called *fufika*. For lack of these things, we used any piece of clothing we managed to get ahold of for further insulation on our bodies. Not having a scarf, I tied some socks together and made a scarf. On the other hand, the socks didn't last very long, so we had to tear up some pants which we wrapped around our feet. The greatest problem was to keep our feet and hands warm. At this point, I don't understand how come we had no presence of mind, or perhaps enough desperation, to demand that the police authorities supply us with these articles. Obviously, it was a known fact that such demands were useless, so we tried the best we could.

The truth of the matter is that as difficult as the situation was for young people, it was extremely difficult for the older men with whom we shared our barrack. These people—the four of them must have been in their sixties at least – spoke German. They were Czech Jews from the Sudeten area in Czechoslovakia. We became very friendly and we tried to help them. They were very old and rather feeble, and one or two did not survive that winter. These people belonged to the upper classes of the Czech officialdom in the Sudetan area, and obviously, that was why they had to flee the German occupation. They found themselves in Poland in 1939, and had to flee from there to Lvov, and that was the place where they were picked up by the Soviets as we were at the same time.

In addition to the cold, we suffered from infestation of body lice. We could not maintain any sanitary standards. It was extremely difficult to have our clothes washed. As a consequence, our daily routine was as follows: We young people went to work. The old men stayed in the house. Upon returning, we cooked food from some meager provisions that the rations gave us, on that tin stove. The problem was to get enough wood for

that stove, since the authorities did not bother to give us any. So we organized teams and we had two people working, say, four hours, followed by
the next team. We had to go out into the night and search for some dead
wood, dead branches, fallen trees, buried in the deep snow. We dragged
the wood to the house, and so we fed the stove all night long. We tried to
bring enough wood in these team relays to last us throughout the day and
night so that the old men could keep themselves warm. After we finished
eating, we got undressed and started searching for lice in our clothing.
That was the daily, or rather nightly, routine Our beds (straw mattresses)
were grouped around the stove to stay as close as possible to the source
of warmth. I managed for a couple of months to somehow get lost from
being accounted for by the police chief – I was not called for work and,
instead, I managed to help the women in our settlement with the secur-
ing of wood for heating. In exchange, I was given some food. I considered
myself fortunate.

That winter, in terms of cold, was the worst I ever experienced. I
do not know the death rate of our co-prisoners, but as I mentioned, one
or two of the older men died that winter. Of course, there was no think-
ing of escaping. We were in one of the most remote areas of Siberia, as I
mentioned before, 800 kilometers to the Trans-Siberian Railroad, and the
distance was covered with impenetrable taiga, pine forest. We did talk
about escaping, but we also realized that any attempt would be completely
unrealistic, in fact, quite mad. Oh yes, there were wolves in the woods.

In the springtime, the police transferred the entire contingent of that
settlement to a new location. These settlements were actually residential
attachments to tremendous mechanical dredges which were excavating
the riverbeds in search of gold. We were transferred to another settlement next to the dredge (in Russian it is called the *Draga*). We took over
the barracks which had been used previously by other prisoners, so they
were in better condition. Also, there was a separate little village where the
Russians were working on that dredge, and lived in the mine cabins. We

had no contact with them. The cold was without any relief, with very low temperatures day after day, with no let up. In fact, winter lasts until about the end of May in that part of Siberia.

Although most of the people were also ordered to cut wood for the mines, somehow I managed to get a special assignment. I became a sledge hammer boy (molotobyets) to a blacksmith. That man was fashioning miscellaneous iron tools and horse shoes for the horses, the main means of locomotion. The work at the smith shop was very heavy. It required quite some strength to raise a heavy hammer, which had to be done in co-ordination with the smithy's more precise work. I also had to tend the fire and run the bellows. The beautiful part of this arrangement was that I was indoors, and consequently I was warm. It also gave me my first opportunity to get close to a Russian. In a very short time, I got to know him quite well. He was a former criminal prisoner who was convicted of slaying someone, and then, after he finished his term of heavy labor, he was ordered, as was customary, to remain in that region supposedly a free man. He took a great liking to me, and I to him. He told me about his family, about his daughter who studied in a medical school, and about the penal system in Russia and how it worked. I liked the work there, but it was much too heavy for me. I had no fresh fruits or vegetables, not enough food altogether, and I was getting weaker and weaker. My body became covered with cysts, and most of them were just under the surface of the skin. They bothered me a lot. Finally, I had to go, and I mean on foot, to a clinic which was at least 15 kilometers away. There a doctor opened some cysts on my shoulder to drain out pus, without using any local anesthesia. It was quite painful, and I still have the scars. I went back to work, but it was no good, I just could not lift that heavy hammer. Eventually, I simply collapsed. They took me to the hospital. As it turned out, the head of the hospital was a Jewish doctor from Moscow, who must have also served some kind of penal term, and he took great interest in and a liking to me. He said in Russian, in his typical, warm-hearted way, "Yossif, I will put you back on your feet," and indeed, he did. Not only that, but he also managed to rid me of a tape worm which had bothered me since childhood. I received a special treat everyday: a bowl of fresh farina with oil; it was delicious. Adequate food, warmth, and the attention of that doctor, put me back on my feet. After several weeks, I went back to work, and I could acquit myself much better.

In the meantime, the great Soviet holiday of May 1st, 1941 came around. We had the day off. As we were sitting in our barrack (it was a huge one with many people), suddenly we heard Russian voices. It turned out that the Russian workers, who also had the day off, decided to take us to their homes to have us celebrate the holiday with them. I was taken to a Russian's home, given food, and then he asked me in his typical, good-natured way, what is it that I would like to have the most? So I said, hesitatingly, "Could you spare a pair of socks?"

He said, "Sure," and believe me, that was one of the best, nicest gifts I ever received. That incident was of great significance to me, because it revealed to me what kind of person the ordinary Russian is. I was not mistaken in my firm belief, which I have until today, that the ordinary Russians by nature are very kind and warm-hearted, willing to help a fellow human being as much as they can. I cannot forget that incident, the whole atmosphere, this warm house with plenty of vodka and herring. We danced the kozatska and all had a good time. Of course, the next day I had a hangover, but it was worth it. It was also the beginning of a great, warm feeling that I developed and still have for the ordinary Russian people.

We continued working, felling trees, cutting them up and and occasionally digging with hand shovels in the bed of streams, and then throwing the dirt onto wooden troughs where water was separating the heavier elements containing gold. I aso had occasion to visit a gold mine, where I saw miners working in unbelievably cramped conditions. They worked gold-bearing seams, perhaps 3 feet in height, so that all the work had to be done lying down. Water was dripping all over the place, and this was where the fruits of our labor went, the timbers to support the mine's ceilings. Of course, the dredges were off limits to anyone except authorized people, and we were told that on an average day, such a dredge could clear, perhaps, 50 kilos of pure gold. Once I did see in the dirt which we were digging out out and throwing into the sluices a gold nugget which, of course, we were not allowed to keep.

And so we worked day after day. We adjusted to the horrible conditions. The weather was getting warmer and spring was upon us. Finally, that fateful day, June 21, 1941, came. We found out that Germany had attacked Russia, and the war now moved East.

In the beginning, this event made no difference to us. We continued working; however, as it turned out, great events, great changes, were in store for us.

As is widely known, after Hitler attacked the Soviet Union, the Western powers, England and the U.S., concluded a pact with Russia of mutual help, and one of the conditions of this normalization of relations was for Russia to recognize the Polish government-in-exile, which was located in London. In addition, Russia also promised to free all the prisoners who they kept in camps who were formerly Polish citizens. That meant my father and me. It took months until this event came about. In the meantime, we were informed of the events on the war front, and these events were ominous. As is known, Germany staged a Blitz Krieg. They found themselves at the gates of Leningrad and Moscow within weeks after the beginning of hostilities. They took Kiev, Charkov, the entire Ukraine, and a good part or European Russia. This situation on the front gave us great fear. At the same time, Russian authorities called us in and told us that we were now free to go wherever we wanted. Of course, there was no thought of going back to Poland, and the decision of most of the people was to go to what was called Central Asia, to the republics of Kazachstan, Kirgistan, Tagikistan, and Uzbekistan (these were Soviet republics north of Afghanistan and not in Siberia proper).

I was in touch with my father by mail, and we made a decision at that time that the best thing would be for him to join me in Aldan. Why did we make this decision? For two reasons. First of all, most of the former prisoners went to Central Asia as a reflex of running away from the cold regions. As it turned out, Central Asia was also very inhospitable to these newcomers, primarily because they were in the midst of epidemics of typhus and dysentery. We found out that a lot of people died there. Later on, many years later, I also found out that a surviving cousin who was in a camp died there. On the other hand, when I was released along wih others, we the young people were given the opportunity to go to Aldan, the second largest town in Yacutia, a town of 10,000 people, and to enroll in a technical institute which was training engineers for the gold industry. We were given, comparatively speaking, very good conditions. We had sleeping accommodations, some clothing, food, and free schooling. I enrolled in that school, together with other young men of my barrack. It seemed to me that Aldan was the place where my father could find some work. After weeks of travelling, my father joined me in the winter of 1941.

At this point, old feelings come to me which have to do with my relationship with my parents, my brothers, and friends. As I said previously, I am a loner, and I wonder if what I mean to say by that is that I can create my own world which will fully occupy me, and satisfy my interests, and my physical and mental and emotional needs, without any recourse to others. I wonder how much of that attitude is due to my experiences during the war.

At home where I lived until I was sixteen, my world revolved around the most important person to me then, my mother, whom I loved and admired. She was very much involved in my life, as well as the life of my brothers. She was the one who knew about any of the problems I might have in school. She was the one who attended the periodic parents; conferences, and she helped me with he Polish compositions, which for some reason gave me a hard time. I thought she was beautiful, intelligent, and charming, and I knew that this was also the opinion of anyone who knew her. I was fond of my brothers, but especially fond of my youngest brother Henio. It was a thrill for me to take him in the morning to his school, which was in the same direction as my school. It was a thrill to hold his hand. He was six years younger. We all took pride in his intelligence. We all thought that he was exceptionally bright. I recall how, sometime before the war, when Henio couldn't be more than six, he started writing a mystery novel, the action taking place on the Riviera in France. We both shared a great interest in collecting stamps. I recall his phenomenal knowledge of geography, and we had a game where his back was the map of Europe, and he said to me, "Scratch me in Paris, or scratch me in Leningrad." I had no doubt that he was an exceptionally gifted child.

With Alex, I had a mixed relationship. He was just a year and a half younger than me, and I always made it a point to make sure to let him know that I was the older one. Consequently, if we played Indians, he had to be the plain Indian, and I had to be the chief. The trouble was that in our games, which also involved our two cousins Leon and Adolph, who had the same relationship age-wise, Leon too insisted on being chief. So all our games consisted of two chiefs lording it over two Indians. I don't think Alex, or for that matter Adolph, liked it very much. What consequences this attitude may have had on our later relationship can only be surmised, and in any case, is not a subject which I want to dwell on here.

My father did not loom very large in my life at that time. We had breakfast together, he came home for lunch, which we had together, and naturally we had dinner together. It was his habit, as was mine too, to read a newspaper or a book while we ate. So there was very little communication during these dining sessions. I knew, on the other hand, that he was a very kind, even-tempered man. The fact is that he never in his life raised his hand against any of us. There is no doubt that three boisterous boys must have been doing some mischievous things which deserved punishment. I do not recall the manner in which we were punished. The greatest treat that my father gave us was usually on a Friday when he brought us either some chocolate or some halvah. Another thing I remember is not receiving any toys, which by the way I did not miss. I made my own toys, boats and airplanes and other items, of wood. I considered my childhood very happy.

I do recall my parents talking about the privations that they had to suffer through during the First World War. I don't know how much that meant to me. I do not know if that was the reason why I was brought up to be self-sufficient, that is, to mend my clothes, help around the house, wash dishes, and be as self-sufficient as possible. The fact is that these abilities were very useful to me when I was on my own without my mother and father. Even today, after having discovered, the hard way, the penalties for loneliness and the beauty of loving someone and being loved in return, I still take great pleasure in being self-sufficient, mostly in small ways. With all this, I am not very clear as to the emotional state I was in, in 1941. No doubt I missed my mother terribly. I do not know if I was kind to others, considerate, or just a loner out to get the most for himself. Well, perhaps not. I do recall that one of the young men in our barrack was definitely a loner, whereas I developed a very warm relationship with a young fellow named Salek. We always worked together, got along very well, and helped each other as much as we could. I also remember the warmth and kindness of he women for whom I was cutting wood, and later on the warmth of the Russians who invited us into their houses. It meant so much to me. Obviously, I was aware of the greatness and beauty of human involvement.

In June 1941, the Germans attacked the Soviet Union. Under pressure, Russia's new ally, the Polish government-in-exile, forced Russia to grant some freedom to Polish exiles. We, of course, benefited. By late 1941, half of Russia was in German hands. Of course, there was no possibility of returning to Poland. Being stuck in Aldan, I could do little to change my circumstances. I took this opportunity to enroll in the local (only) school. Towards the end of 1941, while I was enrolled in the Electro/Mechanical

Technicum (as it was called) of the gold industry, and very much involved in my studies, my father finally joined me. He found a job in a wood-working shop and was given a room. That time of studies I recall with great pleasure. I was especially fond of a couple of my teachers. They were middle-aged Russians. One was an engineer, the other one was formerly an officer in the Czar's army with only one arm, and both men of great intelligence, charm and vast knowledge. They were also "free" men, having served their terms at hard labor for some political transgressions. We did not talk about that. These two men, one teaching physics, the other one math, taught me a lot. Their interests were so wide-ranging that even now I remember how the engineer told us about the great achievement of American industry – the construction of the Hoover Dam, at that time the biggest in the world.

Again, cold winter was upon us and the food supplies that were arriving from far away were getting smaller and smaller. We, the newly released Polish citizens, were given a monthly package of additional food. I recall especially that each one of us received a ration of sugar and milk. I was so starved for carbohydrates that I ate my half pound of sugar, my monthly ration, all at once. My father, however, melted the sugar into caramel and then when I visited him in the evening, he shared it with me. He drank his tea while holding a piece of caramel in his mouth; this way, it lasted longer. In addition to teaching me how to make the sugar last, and how to drink it economically with my tea, my father also revealed to me to me a side of himself which I hadn't known, or suspected. He was willing to share his scarce provisions with me, and our relationship became closer. During that winter, we also saw for the first time the native Yacuts, who came with reindeer to that little town. They were selling reindeer milk, frozen in the shape of bowls. Also they occasionally had hare, which my father cooked and we found delicious. These Yacuts didn't come to town very frequently, and in fact, that was the only winter we saw them. Additional food came some time later, when the horse, which was serving the needs of the school, died of hunger. Each student got a small piece of very tough, stringy meat. We cooked and cooked, and still it was tough. However, it made plenty of soup. With all that, we arrived feeling hunger more and more. I was always waiting until everyone was fed from the common soup kettle, and then we had to wait to see if anything was left. The situation was getting more and more desperate.

There were some small clearings in Taiga cultivated as potato fields (perhaps experimentally), and I remember how we students made forays into these fields some miles away in the middle of the night and dug up some potatoes. Had we been caught, the punishment would have been very severe. Another sign of desperation was when one of the students who displayed artistic talent managed to carve out a stamp, a replica of a bread ration. He himself didn't use it, but he gave it to some of us, and we were successful in getting bread with these faked ration coupons. We shared the bread with him. needless to say, the punishment for getting caught would have been extremely severe. But hunger made us reckless and desperate.

My father's workplace had a lot of wood waste, so my father had this "brilliant" idea of taking these pieces of wood and after working hours while still in the shop to carve cigarette holders. Cigarette holders were a very important item since tobacco was scarce, so that a smoker had to use up the entire cigarette. Cigarettes had no mouthpieces. In fact, all the cigarettes were hand-rolled in a piece of newspaper. A humorous aside, if you asked someone if he had the newspaper (*Pravda*), the answer usually was, "No, I don't smoke." No one considered *Pravda* fit for reading.

My father managed to sell his cigarette holders on the free (illegal) market, and that was considered illegal since he engaged in free enterprise. For the money he got he managed to buy some additional food, which he shared with me. One day he got caught for practicing capitalistic enterprise. By bad luck, just a day or so before his arrest, he had a very bad accident at work on the wood-turning machine, where a piece of wood got loose and flew into his eye, shattered the eyeglass, and as a result he lost sight in one eye. He was arrested the day of the accident, and he asked the arresting officer to be sent to the hospital. Of course, they laughed and he was never sent to a hospital, nor to a doctor. Perhaps, the eye could have been saved.

I received the news of his arrest with great terror. I started running around trying to see different people with some connections to the authorities, to see how my father could be helped. Within a few days, there was a trial. The proverbial troika (three judges) found my father guilty, and he was sent immediately to a labor camp. I started making various attempts to have his case reviewed. I even found a Russian lawyer who promised me that he would make an appeal. In the meantime of course, I lost contact with my father. One day someone gave me a lead, to see a man, also a Polish Jew, who managed somehow to get an important position in the local administration, and I was told that the chief of the NKVD, the Secret Police, could be bribed. I collected my last rubles and gave them to this man, and I was told that he himself, as well as other Polish Jews, would chip in and would give the proper sum to the chief. A week later I got the great news that the appeals court overturned the sentencing of my father and he would be freed. I do not know, as I didn't know at the time, to whom to attribute this miracle. Was it due to the appeal of the lawyer, or was it due to that bribe? But I wasn't really that interested. My main concern was how to see to it that my father was released from prison. I was told that if I followed the normal procedure, it would take a considerable amount of time for the proper documents to reach the prison authorities. On the other hand, if I was willing to take these documents to the prison, and go there on my own, it would speed things up. I chose the second alternative.

The prison was quite a distance away. I had to walk all day long until I finally reached the prison. I asked to see the prison chief. I gave him the papers, he studied them, and obviously convinced of their genuineness, he told me okay, my father would be released when he came back from work. I waited some more. By then night came. Finally the prisoners appeared, my father among them. He saw me, I ran to him with great joy and told him that he was free. He was completely unaware of that fact. He was also unaware of any attempt I was making on his behalf. He was so eager to leave that terrible place that as soon as he was given his bread ration and soup, we decided to go back at night to Aldan.

That trip remains very vivid in my memory. It was a quiet, extremely cold night, everything covered with snow, a narrow roadway leading through the woods. Suddenly, we see a pack of wolves. They did not attack us. They were following us at a distance. We were afraid to stop. We were afraid to make any unusual move, so we kept going, just hoping that they would not attack us. They did not. They just stayed away, but nevertheless, followed us at the same distance almost to the town of Aldan. We finally arrived in the early morning, totally exhausted, but happy with the way events turned out.

As isolated as we were in this far Northeastern corner of Siberia, we knew that the situation on the front was getting worse and worse. The Germans were constantly advancing. Of course, we had no idea about the fate of our families in Poland. We had no idea of what was going on in the rest of the world, whether the Allies were doing anything on other fronts, helping Russia in any way.

In the meantime, a political event came about which also affected our fate, namely, the discovery by the Germans of the mass grave of Polish soldiers in the Katyn forest. The Germans attributed the killing to the Russians, that they killed the Polish officers before the Germans got to them. The Polish government in exile, in London, obviously came to the conclusion that this time the hateful Germans were right in attributing, in blaming the Russians for this atrocity. The Russians naturally denied it. This accusation, corroborated by the Swiss Red Cross, and which the

Polish government accepted, was the basis for a break in diplomatic relations between the Polish government-in-exile and the Soviet Union.

As a result, suddenly we lost our privileged position as Polish citizens. We were told that from then on, we would be treated like everyone else. At once the monthly packages, which we found so helpful, ceased. Our hunger was getting worse by the day. This, combined with the unbearable cold and the isolation of the region, made us decide to appeal to the local authorities to leave the region and permit us to go elsewhere.

CHAPTER 13

To Barnaul (West Siberia), 1943 To 1946

In the spring of 1943, after months of waiting and starving, we received permission to leave the area. We had to find a next transport of trucks which would go to the railroad. We finally made it. We took our meager belongings in some bags and went south to the railroad. We studied the map and decided that the best place to settle would not be Central Asia, which seemed to be the favorite spot for other refugees, but the southernmost part of Siberia, just north of Central Asia, which had a moderate climate with a lot of agricultural areas. And we assumed that the climate would be much better, and the food supply would also be more adequate.

We spent a whole month at that railroad junction waiting for two spots on the Trans-Siberian train that connects Vladivostok with Moscow. There were many others like us eager to go. We finally were permitted to board a train. The train was jammed with people, and the most curious thing I found was that all the food served on the train was American, including noodles. How do I know that it was American? First of all, the bread was white, unheard of in Russia, and the bread was soft—the typical American bread, and of course, this and tea, which was in plentiful supply, already was a great improvement over our previous condition.

After a week of travelling, we arrived in Novosibirsk, which is one of the largest cities of Siberia, close to its western edge. There we got off and again waited for days for a train which would take us south, namely, to a town we decided on by studying the map. That was Barnaul, the capital of another autonomous region, where the native population was supposed to be Altayans. By then our enterprising Polish Jews managed to penetrate most of those towns, and they settle in Barnaul as well, and it was a foregone conclusion that one would help the other in finding accommodation. We developed a network of mutual help through these unofficial semi-underground groupings.

On our arrival in Barnaul, we met some people who told us about an opening for a job for my father in a factory which manufactured dyes for the local textile industry, and for me, a possibility of enrollment in a local technical institute also connected with the textile industry. I turned out that this technicum was newly organized, and all students were girls, so that the director was very eager for more enrollment, and especially of men. I found this director to be a very interesting character. He was a failed poet, I believe. He taught Russian literature. He was full of reminiscences about Mayakovski, Yessenin and other great Russian poets. Besides, he was an alcoholic. He was instrumental in having my father transferred from the dye factory to become the manager of the supply room of his institute. The supply room had rolls of military fabrics, all seconds, which were given to teachers and students to make their clothes. It also had alcohol for a non-existent laboratory and of course, we all knew the fate of that alcohol. The director liked to visit my father in the storeroom. He was a very interesting and unhappy man, this displaced, frustrated poet, seeking oblivion in vodka.

Barnaul was a large city of about 350,000 inhabitants. It even had towards the end of the war years a beginning of a bus service. Life in Barnaul was so different from Aldan, as though we were suddenly transported to a different planet. First of all, we had plenty of potatoes to eat, and bread. There was a flourishing black market where one could buy fruit, which was brought over from Kazakhstan by natives. Barnaul was a place where some of the people from Leningrad managed to get evacuated to, among them the entire Leningrad Symphony Orchestra. So you can imagine my great joy when I was able to attend some concerts of the Leningrad Symphony. I remember, the conductor, Yevgeny Mravinski, who became quite well known later on. I also remember a visit by an operetta company; they gave Lehar's Merry Widow and I fell in love with a dancer, which made me attend the performance more times than I really cared to hear. The love, however, was from a distance. The fact that I was in a mental and physical condition to fall in love already bespoke a lot. During the three miserable years that I spent in Aldan, thoughts of sex and love never even entered my mind, not so in Barnaul. It was a life as close to normalcy as one could expect in these war years in Russia, itself under tremendous assault by the German armies.

Then came the heady days of the great victory in Stalingrad. In Barnaul, as is typical for all towns and settlements in Russia, all the streets and public spaces were wired with loudspeakers, which continually blared music day and night, war bulletins and news from Moscow. (This was not the case in Aldan – too primitive a place.) We were, therefore, quite well informed, at least from the Soviet point of view, about what was going on at the front, especially now since we were about to experience a whole string of victories. It was a tremendous morale booster for us. To backtrack slightly, before that victory in Stalingrad, when things were very bleak, I was told in great confidence by a young Russian friend I acquired whose family was evacuated from the Ukraine, of the following. He told me that one evening when his father, a rather important official, was entertaining some friends, like him also from the Ukraine, they all agreed that the moment the Germans got very close to Barnaul, the first thing they would do, was to kill all the Jews. I couldn't believe my ears. He assured me that he himself would see to it that nothing happened to me, he felt so friendly towards me. Thank God the Germans never came close to Barnaul, and in fact, from 1943 on we rejoiced in one Russian army victory after another. These Russian marshals, Zhukov, Koniev, Rokosofski,

Malenokski, became our greatest heroes. We knew exactly which armies they commanded and which fronts they were on. We lived for that day when the Germans would be smashed.

Our life in Barnaul was so much better for us than the previous one in Aldan, for several reasons. First, the climate. Second, there was food, as primitive as it was, miscellaneous food that filled our stomachs. Not much bread, but a lot of potatoes, and third, we did not feel so isolated from the rest of the world, and we knew what was going on. We also had a modicum of cultural events. I began studying Russian literature in depth. I read all the classics. I then switched to Russian translations of French classics – Victor Hugo, Maupassant, Balzac, Daudet, Anatole France, Jules Romain, and others. I became very friendly with the local librarian who, having gained my confidence and vice versa, let me read some forbidden books. Among them was the Russian translation of Simon Dubnof's book on Jewish history. I also received from her other forbidden books, the titles of which I do not remember.

A very important event in our social life, my father's and mine, occurred when we got to know a Russian Jewish family, whose name now escapes me. The husband was at one time very important in the Communist part of Byelorussia. He was arrested during the purges of the thirties, and sent to Siberia. Obviously whatever befell him had a bad effect on his mental state, because he returned from exile a mentally very disturbed man, I believe melancholic, depressed, and hardly spoke. His wife, however, was a very engaging, pleasant and warm woman. She had a son who was in Moscow and a younger daughter. During the thirties and prior, they were ardent Communists, and important to the establishment. In fact, they named their children in a special way. The son's name was Marlen, which was the combination of the first syllables of Marx and Lenin, and the daughter's name was Iskra, which on one hand means a spark, and on the other hand, it was the name of the first underground newspaper that Lenin published during the Czarist regime. I recall these acts because these people, devoted Communists as they were, were declared enemies or the state in the thirties and exiled to Siberia. By some miracle, they got together, and they settled in Barnaul. From them we discovered the shocking true picture of the purges of the thirties. We were told that all the so-called traitors were simply opponents of Stalin, either standing to the right of him or to the left, and therefore Stalin had to get rid of them, and as we all know, they were executed after mock trials on some phony charges of spying for the Western powers. I recall how especially fond they were (our new friends) of Bucharin, whom they called Bucharinchik, an endearing expression. They said he was a brilliant man. He was executed by Stalin on trumped-up charges. They told us many details of these trials, in great secrecy, and whereas my father was aware of most of these facts, to me it was a revelation. I had to revise my naïve idealistic miscomprehension of what the Soviet regime really represented.

As we all know, the war came to an end on May 8, 1945. The Russians, however, didn't tell us about it until the following day (they suspected that the Western allies might now turn against them and march east into Moscow). When the news reached us that the war was over, that the Germans had surrendered, the entire city population in great joy went out into the streets. I have never seen such an enthusiastic and spontaneous demonstration as on that day. The joy was overwhelming.

Poland was liberated gradually several months prior to that day. We, however, had no news from Poland, we couldn't write, and no mail was coming. After some time, some letters appeared from Poland, but we were not allowed to travel. In the meantime, the Soviet government, under pressure from the United States and England, and as a result of agreements which were concluded in Yalta, agreed to allow the setting up of a coalition government in liberated Poland. They also agreed to the repatriation of all Polish citizens back to Poland. Committees were organized, and we were all waiting patiently for the word when we would be allowed to return to our homes. Among those waiting were not only the

Jews who escaped, but also Poles, that is, Christians who were arrested by the Russians in the eastern part of Poland. They, too, were given permission, eventually under proper conditions, to return to Poland.

It took a full year after the end of the war for the first transports to leave the Soviet Union. Finally, our turn came. We were all in a fraternal, holiday mood as we boarded the freight trains. Now, being free citizens, we made them as comfortable as we could, and we were provided with enough food. Finally, in May or so of 1946, our train started moving west. The trainload of people, Jews and Gentiles, burst out in Polish patriotic songs. Our train had to give right of passage to military transports going in all directions. We started meeting trainloads of civilian people who were forcibly transported from the Western part of Russia, Byelorussia and the Ukraine to Siberia. Here we go again! – but now that was happening to the inhabitants of these areas which were occupied by the Germans. This German occupation "contaminated" the local population. The Russian authorities started arresting thousands of people, Ukrainians, Byelorussians, Tartars, Volga Germans, and many other minorities, and shipping them to Siberia.

We, on the other hand, newly liberated, were going west to Poland. We also started coming across trainloads of German prisoners of war going east to Siberia, or trainloads of Japanese prisoners of war going west. As a result, it took us a long time to reach the Moscow rail hub. There, with the train on the siding, and told that the train would stay a couple of days in Moscow until the way was cleared to continue the trip west, my father and I jumped out of the train, and we went sightseeing to Moscow. We managed to visit the Tretyakovski Gallery of Art, Red Square, with the Kremlin behind the wall, the Gum department store (the biggest in Russia), the Moscow River, and of course, Lenin's mausoleum. In the evening, we were back in our train. The next day, we continued on our westward journey.

The trainload of people, both Jews and Poles, maintained what appeared to be a very friendly relationship. We sang Polish patriotic songs, exchanged tales of our war years, and otherwise maintained a normal, friendly atmosphere. Everything was fine, and the trains were rolling westward, until we came to within a short distance of the Polish border. Then, suddenly, a very strange thing happened. Up to now the Poles and the Jews were intermingled in the railroad cars; suddenly the Poles left the predominantly Jewish cars, and the Jews were told to leave the predominantly Polish cars, so that the train had now exclusively Jewish cars and Polish cars. To make sure that whoever wanted to know which were the Polish cars, the Poles started putting on crosses and holy pictures of the Madonna, Holy Mary, outside their doors. It was not a pleasant turn of events. Its significance escaped me at the time.

CHAPTER 14

Returning to Poland, Spring 1946

We finally came to the Polish border, and crossing the same, stopped in a small Polish town. Eagerly, my father and I jumped out of the train and went into the town, which was quite nearby, to say hello to the people and share the joy or our coming to our "motherland."

The Poles we encountered suddenly turned against us. They said, "Ah, the Jews are back," and they started throwing stones at us. We quickly turned around and ran back to the train. I somehow lingered behind, not really believing what I was seeing I finally managed to reach the train under a hail of stones, and quickly the people pulled me in and closed the big sliding door. The stones made a depressing racket on that door. This was our welcome back committee organized by the "friendly" Polish population.

In recalling this time, I still get a feeling of great depression. Little did we know at that time what was in store for all of us, and what was in store especially for me personally. We saw soon enough that we had entered an overwhelming sea of hatred. The situation in Poland was extremely volatile and unstable. The government imposed by Russia, on the surface a coalition, really had no popular support. The rightwing elements, which also formed a part of the underground army during the German occupation, continued underground activities against the Russian army, as well as against the Polish units of the police or army. As our train kept rolling further west, and finally entered the former German territories of Pomerania, we kept hearing every night the sounds of machine gun fire. Obviously, the Russians were battling the Polish underground units. One night the sounds of battle were right next to our train. We locked the doors, and we were there, sitting and shivering, apprehensive about our safety. Finally, the train came to a stop, and we found ourselves in the former German city, Stettin, renamed by the Poles, Szczecin. That town, a large port city on the Baltic sea, was considerably destroyed by Allied bombing, and the entire German population was driven out by the Russians. We were told that we could have any apartment we wished in the surviving buildings. We then went from building to building (by the way, the buildings were interconnected through the cellars), and there we found roomfuls of abandoned fine furniture left by the Germans. We quickly furnished for ourselves a beautiful apartment overlooking either a beautiful square or the sea, a truly great accommodation one can only dream about. Came the night, however, we had to close the doors and windows in our apartment, because there was shooting going on constantly. We felt very threatened by the situation, and there was a growing conviction among all of those refugees that there was no future whatsoever in Szczecin, and that in order to feel more secure, we should all rejoin the large Jewish centers in Warsaw, Lodz or Wroclaw.

We decided to take a train to Lodz, and we abandoned all these luxuries for the sake of safety. Upon arrival in Lodz we were taken in hand by representatives of a Jewish committee, and were given some very primitive accommodations, primitive but safe. The Jewish quarter of Lodz was completely demolished, we were told, by the Poles after the Jews were taken out of the ghetto by the Germans. The Poles simply demolished the ghetto in search of hidden treasures, we were told. Lodz was filled with thousands upon thousands of newcomers like us, searching for a place to live, or a place to work, or for younger people, perhaps to study. The outlook was bleak. Our contact with the Poles was non-existent. We felt secure only among ourselves, Jews. We were hoping that, perhaps, soon after the coming which was slated for some day in June, 1946, where the Poles were supposed to decide on the form of government that they wanted, that the situation would settle down, it would become more secure. The election day came, and we decided that now, hopefully matters would calm down, and there would be great security. We also decided that it would be wise for me, without my father, to travel to Kielce in order to find out whatever I could about my mother and brothers.

CHAPTER 15

Going to Kielce,
July, 1946 – Pogrom Follows

Several days prior to my departure, we happened to find an old friend of my father's from Kielce, a fellow Bundist, who had been in Poland for several months. He greeted us and gave us whatever information he had about the liquidation of the ghetto in Kielce. I recall the moment vividly. My father and I asked this man what he knew if anything about the fate of our mother and brothers, and he told us that in 1942, according to his information, they were sent out along with the entire Jewish population to an extermination camp, Treblinka. He said all this in what appeared to me to be a very matter-of-fact, unemotional way.

I turned around and I ran away, and there, standing in a dark hallway, I cried, probably for the first time in many, many years. Mr. S., our informant, made it unmistakably clear for us that there was no need, there was no reason, to hope for a miracle. My mother and brothers were dead.

The decision for me to travel to Kielce still held. There I could gather firsthand, additional information about my vanished family. A day before departure, I ran into an old friend, whom I knew in my high school days, Zev Zilberberg, who decided to join me in our travel to Kielce. On July 4, 1946, very early in the morning, we boarded the train. We arrived at daybreak and started looking for the building housing the local Jewish committee (the presence of which was typical for all these Jewish towns where the returning Jews managed to set up a focal point, as well as a means of finding security and a roof over their heads). The first thing we did, Zev and I, was to walk along the main street of the town Sienkiewicza Street, to the very end. The town seemed so small – I either had grown bigger or the town had shrunk. Having seen the main drag of the town, we came back to the building housing the Jewish Committee. That building, a two-story structure, was off the center of town on the edge of a small canal. Upon arriving, we were greeted warmly by the other people staying there, and given some food, and we proceeded to wash up. After a certain interval, we heard shouting from the outside. Soon after, we heard stones being thrown at the building. We looked out the window, and there was a crowd of people outside, getting larger and larger and throwing stones at us, smashing windows, and shouting some incomprehensible demands or obscenities. I was puzzled, but tried to find out the reason for all that commotion. We were told not to worry, that at the door to our house was a Polish policeman with his machine gun, and he would make sure that no one threatened our security.

We soon found out from the shouts that the Poles gathered outside were accusing us of either harboring or killing a young Polish boy. We were afraid to go to the windows, because the hail of stones was getting thicker. When I did manage to look out, I saw that the crowd gathering outside, in a huge square, was tremendous. Suddenly we heard further commotion at the entrance door, and running steps. It became clear that the crowd had either overwhelmed the policeman, or he most likely simply gave up and let the people in. The Jews inside, and there must have been close to 50 people, men, women and children, ran up to the second floor pursued by the crowd. We finally ran to the last room, where all of us crowded into a dormitory room and squeezed ourselves on top, under and in between the beds. There, we packed ourselves inside the small space, barricaded the door, and prayed for a miracle.

After a moment, we heard banging on the door, and shouts of, "Come out or we will throw a grenade. All of you will be killed." People started screaming. There was a young man among us who had a gun, and he said he was going to use it on the attackers. We pleaded with him not to provoke the crowd. They finally broke the door down and started dragging us out of the room, forcing us to leave the building with our hands up. They obviously had good training in Hitler's methods. I, among others, was lead down the stairs and into the open square with my arms up in the air. At this point, in sheer desperation, and relying on my Aryan Polish appearance, I lowered my arms and wiggled in between the legs of the crowd, hoping to make myself invisible and disappear among them. Suddenly, I felt people's arms on me. They started shouting at me, "You're a Jew. We saw you coming down from the house."

I said, "No, no, I am not."

One said "No, you can't fool us. We saw you among them, so you must be a Jew."

At this point, I broke down, I started crying, begging them to let me go, saying, "So what if I am a Jew, what do you want from me? I haven't done anything to you." I didn't have much of a chance to plead. The next thing I remembered, I was lying on the ground, and something wet and warm was caking over my eyes. Some time later, I remember opening my eyes, seeing people, nurses, asking if my friend Zev was there, and then again, losing consciousness. I regained consciousness some days later after all the survivors were taken to a hospital in Lodz.

This was the famous pogrom in Kielce on July 4, 1946. The world knew very little about it. Let's not forget that the Western allies were still friends with Russia. The news of a pogrom in liberated Poland in 1946, when more than 45 people, Jews, were killed by the freedom-loving Poles, would have been unbelievable to the entire world. Oh yes, the *Times* saw fit to print a small notice on the front page, and I managed to get a copy of this many years later. The fact is that when I talk to many people, intelligent, well-read, caring people and ask if they ever heard of a pogrom in Poland after the war, no one knew of that event. Even now it is still shocking to a lot of people to find out that so many Jews were killed a year or more after the collapse of the Nazis, and not by the Nazis!

Sometime later, we were given some information about what happened in Kielce. It was a typical libel of ritual murder repeated so many times in the history of the Jews in the last two thousand years. The Jews were accused of killing a Polish boy for the sake of extracting blood for matzos. Of course, July is quite removed in time from Passover, which was the usual time when Jews were accused of performing such atrocities in order to obtain blood, the necessary ingredient for proper matzos. But one doesn't need many excuses for barbaric acts. Obviously, the Polish authorities, if they did have any serious thoughts of defending us, were overwhelmed. The reason I survived, along with over 20 people in that town, was because I lost consciousness after being hit over the head with a hard object; the murderers obviously assumed that I was dead. Towards the evening, when additional police or military forces came from other towns to restore order, they threw all the bodies onto trucks, and at that point they discovered that I was still alive. I was taken to the hospital (St. Alexander), which was a short distance from the public school I went to, and not far from where we had our dream house that we had built in the thirties. After two or three days, we were transferred to a former German hospital in Lodz, where we were given the utmost care.

I must mention at this point what all this meant to my father. He didn't go with me because he looked too Jewish. He assumed that my Polish appearance would keep me safe. When the news came to him about the pogrom in Kielce, he was beside himself with fear. There was talk about organizing the relatives of the Jews in Kielce, and sending them to the hospital to recognize any survivors (or the dead, for that matter), but those people, my father among them, were not allowed to go. Instead, they were assured that the survivors would be brought back to Lodz. No one knew the names of most of the survivors. When I came to Kielce with Zev, we had no chance to sign our names or otherwise identify ourselves.

When the survivors were brought to Lodz, my father, after being admitted to the hospital, ran from one patient to the other trying to divine from under these bloody bandages, who his son was. He finally ascertained that I was one of the survivors. When I regained consciousness for a short time, my father was there next to me. My consciousness returned to me for longer and longer durations. However, it took me two or three weeks before I could speak. I suffered a very severe brain concussion. I finally recovered after several weeks of very good medical care and attention. Being still very weak and wobbly, with continuous dizzy spells, I was allowed to join a young people's camp in Silesia. This camp was run and controlled by Zionists whose purpose was to prepare us for immigration to Palestine. My purpose in that camp was to recover and regain my strength. After four weeks, I rejoined my father in Lodz.

One day, out of the blue, we received a letter from the U.S. It was sent by our uncle and aunt, Meyer and Reggie Silverstein, to whom we wrote shortly after arriving in Poland. We did not remember their address in New York, and therefore our letter was simply addressed to "Mr. & Mrs. Silverstein, NYC." Those were the times when the American post office still managed to perform miracles. The letter found its recipient. And so, soon after settling in Lodz and soon after my return from camp, came this great letter. In the letter we were told that my brother, Alex, survived the holocaust, along with our cousins, Leon and Franka, and that the three of them were in a displaced persons' camp in Germany, in the American-occupied zone. It was a miracle. Simultaneously, with this news, we met some people, and a woman among them looked at me closely, and not knowing my name, said to me, "Do you by any chance have a brother in a DP camp in Germany?"

At that time, I had already found out that this was so, nevertheless, this confirmation was the second miracle. I never considered that I looked anything like my brother, and yet this woman saw a definite family resemblance. We immediately sent off a letter to Alex, and soon after received a reply from him, along with a photo of him and of our cousins Leon and Franka, survivors like him of the horrors of the ghetto and the Nazi extermination camps. When I regained my strength, we, my father and I, decided that the only thing left for us to do would be to join Alex in the DP camp.

Let me explain at this point, the overall situation in Europe, and in particular, Poland. The pogrom in Kielce had a devastating effect on any prospects that the Jewish population, those who survived the concentration camp, and those who were returning from Russia, could fulfill their dreams of re-establishing their lives in Poland. The pogrom which claimed so many lives, was just another incident, another fragment in a vicious campaign launched by the Poles against the returning Jews. Perhaps it was caused by their fear that the Jews would reclaim their properties, apartments, businesses. Perhaps there were other, to me unfathomable reasons; nevertheless, the point was made abundantly clear that the Jews were not welcome in Poland, that they could consider Poland only as a passing phase, and must seek life elsewhere. Thousands upon thousands of Jews who found themselves in Poland started running away.

CHAPTER 16

Going to a Displaced Persons Camp in Germany, 1947

Many years later I found out that my uncle Jacob, my mother's younger brother, who had survived the war years far into Russia, where his family had grown to three daughters, along with many others had also decided to return to Poland. The news of the pogrom in Kielce reached them as they crossed the Polish border. The panic that ensued made them turn around, and the Russian authorities allowed them to return to the place where they came from. Most of the Polish Jews decided to run any place where they were welcome and even where they were not welcome, as long as it was secure. No one could go to Palestine in a direct way. No one could go, for that matter, to the German DP camps.

We found that the American Joint Distribution Committee, along with many other organizations, managed by hook or by crook to organize the exodus from Poland of large groups. My father and I decided to join such a group. In the fall of 1946, we were taken at night across the border between Poland and Czechoslovakia. There other activists met us, told us to get rid of any evidence that any of us ever was in Russia, and then we boarded the train. At that time, Czechoslovakia was in full control of the Russian army. Obviously, this transport was well organized, as were many others, and we were allowed to travel across Czechoslovakia and then cross the border to Austria. We arrived in Vienna, and were placed in a huge refugee center, which in the past, we were told, was the palatial residence of one of the Rothschilds. The main concern was sanitation and health. Every man had to drop his pants and was given a powdery application of DDT. After a couple of days in Vienna, we were shipped to another settlement, this one in Puch, a small village in the Austrian Alps, not far from Salzburg. We spent a whole month in that camp waiting for a transport, which would take us across the Austrian-German border to Germany. We finally arrived in a town named Landshut, Bavaria.

There, while our train, consisting of great numbers of cars with doors wide open, was moving very slowly from one siding to another, a miracle happened. There was another train loaded with refugees going in the opposite direction, very slowly, and then, as my father and I were sitting on the edge of the car, we saw in the car across, moving in the opposite direction, my uncle Moishe. My father recognized him, called his name. He recognized us too, but the trains were moving. Finally, both trains came to a halt. We then jumped out and ran into each other's arms. That was the second and last survivor of my mother's huge family.

We stayed in Landshut several days waiting for the arrival of Alex and Leon. Finally, they arrived. We somehow recognized each other. This first encounter remains vividly in my mind. I must say that the encounter was reserved. I don't know why we didn't run into each other's arms. We didn't jump for joy. I recall Alex taking off his shirt and washing up outdoors, and I was impressed with his hairy chest. I had hardly any hair on my chest. He had grown and become so much more mature. To reinforce this, I remember Alex saying to me, "You have such a thin voice." That night was the only time since we met again, that Alex told us what happened in the ghetto, and what happened to him after that. I cannot repeat at this point what he said to us. It is a subject that I find very difficult to think about, and no doubt, so does Alex. We never since broached the subject. Many thoughts since that encounter entered my mind about

Alex, about my mother, and my youngest brother. I put myself in their shoes, and especially, in Alex's shoes, to help understand my own feelings, as well as his. The feelings of guilt that I have, which I cannot overcome, are still with me. Alex never reproached me for being abandoned by his father, or by his older brother, or for anything else that he had to live through and survive. He didn't reproach me, but he didn't have to. I know, this was fate. I find it difficult to dwell even now on the subject.

Alex and Leon managed, in spite of great difficulties, to take us on a train to the displaced persons camp where they were staying. It was a settlement called Zeilsheim near Hoehst, outside of Frankfurt am Main. We were there under the care of UNRRA, the United Nations Refugee Organization. My father was allowed to join his sister, Reggie, in the winter of 1946. A year later, it was Alex's, Leon's, and Franka's turn to go by boat to the States. My turn came nine months later, when finally on August 18, 1948, I disembarked in New York Harbor from the Liberty ship, Marine Swallow, and there I was greeted by all my regained and new family, and where I started a new life in the United States.

CHAPTER 17

The Music Returns

When I left the Soviet Union in 1946 at the ripe old age of 23, I realized that an important part of my life was over: my childhood, the loss of my mother and her love, my childhood friends, my Yiddish and Polish culture, especially music. I tried to accommodate myself to the new life. I started to voraciously read English books and magazines, dance the American hits, which were so popular in the American forces network of the U.S. Army, and attend the "serious" concerts of Frankfurt's Philharmonic. Yes, before the war I had been preoccupied with doing the best in school subjects—math, physics, history both present and ancient, current events, the war in Spain, foreign language (English), anything else that was written about, and of course, music.

Coming home, I would rush to my mother to tell her about the song I just heard. We both sang it together. In turn, she sang a new song she just heard. She had a lovely voice and sang light songs during the family's Thursday night gatherings. I tried to accompany her on my violin.

Now, it seemed, music, and the violin, was returning to my life, along with a somewhat pleasurable social life. While in the DP Camp, I established long-lasting friendships with numerous survivors with similar backgrounds. Some resulted in romantic relationships—and not all of them successful. When, 30 years later, I happened to meet some survivors, they all remembered the old events.

CHAPTER 18

Arriving in New York

The day I arrived in New York, I still remember seeing the Statue of Liberty and all the cars on the drive to Brooklyn below. I never saw so many cars, it was so busy. My first day in America was one of the most thrilling days of my life.

I was greeted warmly by everyone, including my cousins and Aunt Rivka and Uncle Meyer. They lived on Vermilaey Avenue in Washington Heights. Uncle Meyer took charge. He said, "First we are going to the barber on Broadway to make you look more American." Then he took me to the local haberdashery, and bought me an outfit, everything. My transformation to American was quick and painless.

Right away we were taken care of by the Society for New Americans at 15 Park Row. They found us an apartment for us in Brooklyn on Kingston Avenue. It was more than adequate for the three of us. The Society provided us with some clothing and funds to buy food. At this point, Alex and I decided we would stop speaking Polish and focus on English. We read two liberal newspapers—one was the *Post*.

People would ask me, 'What do you want to do for work? What do you want to be?" I told them, an architect.

I was told that since you have no money, you can go to Cooper Union if you pass the exam. First, I took all the required high school subjects, and after two years, graduated and got my diploma. Then, I went to night school after working all day in a printing shop. After two years, I was glad to leave the printing field. I started work in an architectural firm, and was admitted after passing qualification tests.

I attended Cooper Union night school from 1950 to 1954. We would go out after classes and drink at McSorley's Bar, and I became friendly with some fellow students there. One couple, Frank and his wife Jean, introduced me to wonderful Italian food, and we remained friends for many years. After Cooper Union, I attended Columbia University School of Architecture from 1955 to 1958, two years at night, and one during the day.

I started to search for a job in architecture. It was hard to get, but I eventually came to Charles Spindler's firm in Brooklyn. They were dedicated to designing gas stations and upgrading heating systems in buildings. I became very good at that work. The office felt like a group of friends.

One day I went to a meeting in the City Buildings Department. My boss, Mr. Spindler, was there. Afterward, he invited me to lunch on Montague Street. I was flattered. We went up to the second floor—the whole office was there and they applauded me. Why? I had just become an American citizen and that was something to be celebrated.

CHAPTER 19

Meeting President Truman, 1953

In the next years, we—Alex, Leon, a friend, and I— took our yearly vacations to explore our new country. We bought a used car and headed out, north to New England, including Maine, south to Washington, DC, North Carolina, the Blue Ridge Mountains, Tennessee, and further west to Missouri, Kansas, Colorado, and the mountains and federal parks there.

It was 1953, with. Eisenhower as the new president. Truman was in retirement in Kansas City. Having arrived in Kansas City, we asked a policeman where Truman had his office. He sent us to the Federal Bank Building. We went right in, to Truman's floor, and met the receptionist in the plain, unassuming office.

"We are new Americans and we are exploring the USA. We would like to see President Truman," we announced. I knew he had something to do with helping refugees.

"Well, he is dictating his memoir, come back in an hour," she said. We came back and waited. No one else was there.

The door opened. "Hello fellows, you are new Americans?" He seemed so big to me. He stretched out his arms and ushered us into his office. "What made you come here?"

We told him we were exploring our new country, and he told us what we should be sure to see on our trip.

"You are from Poland," he said. "Stalin double-crossed me. He promised me Poland would be a free country, and then he didn't do what we agreed to do." He reached into his desk and gave us each a coin with a Missouri mule on one side. He was a very warm man and we enjoyed chatting with him.

The whole interview lasted ten minutes. He had no pretensions and we could see that he understood our sentiments.

CHAPTER 20

My Marriage and Filming Joe's Violin

I carried many cultural interests with me to my new home in America. They were nourished by attending concerts, exhibits, and exploratory walks. Back in the days when the Museum of the City of New York held walks, I joined a walk to explore the mansions of the Upper East Side. There I met this girl named Regina on the steps of the Carnegie Mansion, and on our walk, I ventured to ask her for a first date.

Alex had some tickets for the Metropolitan Opera, and we went to see *The Magic Flute*. Thereafter, we went to restaurants and visited each other's homes. After three months, we agreed to marry. The wedding was at Regina's home on West End Avenue. This was the start of a most happy chapter in my life. I also gained a new, extended family, including Regina's two daughters, Karen and Ame.

A few months after the wedding, we bought a second home, an old house upstate in Ghent, Columbia County, New York. The ceilings were low, not more than seven feet. *We can make it better,* I convinced Regina. I removed part of the living room ceiling and created a balcony. A big piece of the ceiling almost fell on us. But my motto was, if I could do it myself, I would. It took several years to make the place livable, which also involved a lot of landscaping.

I liked to put our weekend guests from the city to work, including Ame and her high school friends. One time she brought a guy and I showed him a big tree. "Can you help me cut this down?" I asked him. Ame said, "See? I told you he would ask you to do that."

I put to good use whatever I learned before coming to America. I knew about cutting down trees and construction from the labor camps. I loved the fields and forests, and the Vistula River. I inherited my knowledge of nature and the landscape from my mother, and it stayed with me all my life.

Regina and I continued to explore the city, visit museums, and attend concerts as often as we could. I also always found time to play my violin or listen to music. But after many years, Regina became ill and I had to take care of her. We didn't get out so much. Over time, my fingers grew stiff with age and arthritis, and I found it harder and harder to play the violin. Finally, I put it away in its case. It seemed inevitable. My relationship with this violin was over. Or, so I thought.

Regina and Joe in Ghent, New York.

Joe and Regina's home in Ghent. It reminded him of his childhood home in Poland.

Drawing by Joseph Feingold, Architect in New York City.

CHAPTER 21

Joe's Violin Continues... an Afterword

BY SHEILA LEWIS

The rest, as they say, is history. The film Joe's Violin can be seen online. Joseph Feingold is my uncle, and his late wife Regina was the youngest sister of my father, Morris Kaufman. Joe's original autobiography and the film offer an inspiring American immigrant story that spans generations and cultures. Parents and grandparents love to share Joe's story with their children, especially because it takes the difficult and unfathomable subject of the Holocaust in a different direction.

Its message, with descriptions of the horrors and privations of imprisonment, displacement, and anti-Semitism, is ultimately one of hope, renewal, and survival. Although not originally intended as such, Joe's story now has timely political overtones. In a recent interview, he shared his concern about the plight of refugees today. "In America, I was welcomed with open arms. What would have happened if they hadn't taken me in?"

Joe was known as a hard worker and a successful architect. He loved his country property in Ghent, New York. The roughly 16 acres of land were an unruly tangle of bramble and fields that seemed to stretch for miles before Joe (and any willing visitors) tamed them.

After a long day of labor, Joe liked to play his fiddle, as he called it, by the fireplace. He didn't speak much of his World War II years, his time in Siberia, and his various daring escapades. Thankfully, as he mentioned in the beginning of this book, Joe wrote his memoir in 1985, and invited anyone who was interested to read it. The new chapters added to Joe's original autobiography add another tuneful chord to the story, like the music he always loved.

The original *Autobiography of Jozef Fajngold* ends with Joe's exhilarating first day in America. After the usual immigrant struggles, things went uphill, culminating in his thriving career and happy life with Regina. His story includes the "unimaginable ways" Joe's life has changed since the film was made. He is in touch with the film's family, new friends, and fans.

Brianna, whose parents were immigrants from the Dominican Republic, played the violin for Denzel Washington at an Academy Awards party. In July, 2017, she and Joe talked about the benefits of their intergenerational friendship as guests at a UN conference.

The film was shown several times in Joe's Upper West Side neighborhood. Audiences were always moved to tears. During Holocaust Remembrance Week in April, 2017, Joe, Brianna, and her music teachers were united at a screening and concert at Ansche Chesed, the nearby synagogue I attend. The next evening, Joe and producer Raphaela Neihausen and Kahane Cooperman spoke at a sold-out screening at the JCC Film Center, two blocks from Joe's home. Finally, the next morning, Joe was videotaped in his apartment for the U.S. Holocaust Memorial Museum's archives. His story will unfold for future visitors to the museum, which is located in Washington, DC.

In July, 2017, *Joe's Violin* appeared on PBS/POV (Public Television's Point of View series). In August, 2017, Joe was interviewed and videotaped by the USC (University of Southern California) Shoah Foundation Holocaust Awareness Institute.

Joe listens daily to WQXR, his favorite classical music station. He continues to share his story with visitors and students from nearby schools, just as he did with Ame, her sons, his three nephews, and friends and extended family years ago. Each time Joe tells it, a fresh note across time and space emerges. Listeners may hear their own family's story echoing, somehow, through his.

I didn't give away the violin because it didn't mean anything.

Joseph Feingold and his famous violin at home, 2017. (photo: Mark Feingold)

I gave it away because it meant so much.

Brianna Perez and Joe, 2017

Brianna and Joe

Brianna, Joe, and Kokoe Tanaka-Suwan

Holocaust Memorial event at Ansche Chesed, with Brianna,
Rabbi Jeremy Kalmanofsky, Joe, and Kokoe. (photo: Sheila Lewis)

Sheila Lewis, Brianna, Joe, and Kokoe,
April 2017 event for Holocaust Memorial.

Passing the baton, or violin, from Brianna to Nya,
with film producers Raphaela Neihausen and Kahane Cooperman.

Joe and Brianna

Good news: Oscar nomination announced! Kokoe, Joe, and Brianna.

On the red carpet with Joe's Violin: Raphaela, Brianna, Kahane, and Kokoe.

TIMELINE AND CHRONOLOGY OF EVENTS

1. Jozef Fajngold was born in Warsaw, Poland on March 23, 1923. His parents were Aron Shloime (Aaron) and Ruchle Laya (Rachel), nee Jakubowski. His brother Alex was born in 1924. Brother Henry, born in 1929, perished in Treblinka in 1942.
2. The family moved to Kielce in 1933.
3. They moved to Lvov, eastern Poland, in 1939.
4. Joe was sent by the Russians to Siberia in 1940.
5. He stayed first in the Aldan labor camp (Siberia) until 1943.
6. Joe was then sent to the Barnaul labor camp in 1946.
7. He returned to Poland in the spring of 1946, first to Stettin, then to Lodz.
8. After returning to Kielce to check on his family home, Joe was injured in the infamous Kielce pogrom on July 4, 1946.
9. Finding out that Alex had survived Auschwitz, Joe and his father joined Alex at the displaced person's camp, in Zeilsheim, Germany.
10. Joe's father was admitted to the U.S. at the end of 1947, and Joe followed in the summer of 1948.
11. Joe settled in New York, first in Brooklyn with Aron and Alex, and eventually in Manhattan.
12. His first job was at a printing company as a hand printer. After that, he found work in architectural offices.
13. He attended night school at Cooper Union from 1950 to 1954.

14. Joe, Alex, and Leo went on a vacation trip in 1953, where they met former President Truman in his Missouri office.

15. Joe was admitted to Columbia University's School of Architecture in 1955 and graduated in 1958.

16. He received his license to practice architecture in 1963.

17. Joe started work at his own architecture firm in a brownstone on West 78th Street, New York City, in 1962, where he remained until retirement in 2010.

18. Joe married Regina (nee Kaufman) in June, 1971. They met on a walking tour at the Museum of the City of New York.

19. Joe and Regina bought an old house and farm upstate in Ghent, New York in 1971. They added acreage, enlarged the house, and Joe did the renovation.

20. The couple moved to East 70th street, where they lived until 2008.

21. Joe wrote the autobiography of Jozef Fajngold in 1985.

22. Joe and Regina moved to the Esplanade residence on West End Avenue in 2008.

23. Joe donated the violin he purchased in a German DP camp in 1946 to the WQXR music drive in March, 2014.

24. Kahane Cooperman started to work on the documentary, *Joe's Violin*, soon after the music drive.

25. Regina died in October, 2015, after a long illness.

26. *Joe's Violin* received an Oscar nomination for best short documentary film in February, 2017.

27. Many articles, news spots on TV and radio, interviews and videotapes were written and broadcast from 2015 to the present. Now archived are videotapes at the U.S. Holocaust Museum in Washington, DC, and the University of Southern California's Shoah Foundation Institute.

28. *Joe's Violin* was screened, sometimes with live appearances and presentations, at film festivals around the country and abroad since its first public screenings in April, 2016.

29. The film aired on the PBS/POV (public television point of view) series in July, 2017. It won an audience choice award at the Berkshire Jewish Film Festival, in the summer of 2017.

30. Joe and Brianna Perez, the student who was first chosen to play the violin, were guest speakers at a U.N. Conference on Intergenerational Friendship.

VIEW THE FILM AND FIND OUT MORE
AT WWW.JOESVIOLIN.COM

For information about related programming, contact:
Sheila Lewis at sheilaklewis@gmail.com

Send mail correspondence to:
Joseph Feingold, 305 West End Ave., Apt. 1207, New York, NY 10023

ACKNOWLEDGMENTS

Many people have helped this book reach fruition with their dedicated and hard work. I especially want to thank:

My friends and family for their encouragement and continued loving support.

Editorial Team: Sheila Lewis, my dear niece, for her interviews, editing, and expert ability to bring together the strands from my past and present into one voice and story. This book would not have happened without her; Phyllis Stern, for her excellent copyediting and manuscript preparation, and her thoughtful questions; Mark Feingold, my dear nephew, for preparing the photographs that greatly enhance the portrayal of events in this book; Sharon Pelletier, for her time and advice on making the story and its structure better and stronger; Rob Siders of 52 Novels, for the beautiful design and layout.

Joe's Violin Family: Kahane Cooperman, the amazing filmmaker and co-producer who first envisioned this film, and talented co-producer Raphaela Neihausen—together with their crew they worked tirelessly to shape the destiny of this film. Special thanks go to music teachers and violinists Kokoe Tanaka Suwan and Hannah van der Swaagh, and to the lovely Brianna Perez, whose friendship means so much; the Bronx Global Learning Institute for Girls; Kathleen of the Mr. Holland's Opus Foundation and the WQXR music drive crew, for finding a new home for my violin. All of them have brought joy to many people, new life to me, and a happy ending to this story.